Organise Yourself!

This book belongs
to
MR & MRS MACKAY
DRUMDUIE BOGALLAN
NORTH KESSOCK
ROSSSHIRE
IV1 1XE

Ann R. Thomas

Roe Deer

Organise Yourself!

RONNIE EISENBERG with KATE KELLY

PIATKUS

© 1997 Ronni Eisenberg with Kate Kelley

First published in Great Britain in 1986 by
Judy Piatkus (Publishers) Limited
5 Windmill Street
London W1P 1HF

This edition revised and updated 1997

First published in the United States in 1986 by
MACMILLAN, a Simon & Schuster Macmillan company

The moral right of the author has been asserted

*A catalogue record for this book is available
from the British Library*

ISBN 0 7499 1769 5

Data capture and manipulation by
Phoenix Photosetting, Chatham, Kent
Printed and bound in Great Britain by
Mackays of Chatham PLC, Chatham, Kent

CONTENTS

INTRODUCTION

In the eleven years since I wrote *Organise Yourself!*, our world has changed a great deal. Today we are overwhelmed by voluminous amounts of e-mail as well as regular mail; we have fax machines spewing out paper so fast that the pages seem to be begging to be read instantly; and electronic organisers or calendars on laptop computers have often replaced diaries.

The world also offers more options for making life convenient. Today we can have our salary deposited directly into our bank account, and we can leave a standing order for payment on some of the regular bills, or if we prefer, we can pay our debts electronically from the comfort of our own computer screen. The latest phone systems offer terrific features that make life easier, and computers and those paper-spewing faxes are actually real time-savers when used properly.

When I thought about all the changes that needed to be incorporated to bring the book into the twenty-first century, I also thought about another thing: the basic advice for getting organised still stands the test of time. I'm going to be showing you how to take the principles I wrote about eleven years ago and apply them to our world today.

People's concern about getting more control over their lives has also remained constant. I still get the same response when I tell people that I make my living teaching others how to become better organised. 'Boy, could I use you!' is what I hear. Often that comment is followed by a sigh and a true confession: 'Organising takes too much time. I just can't be bothered.' Other familiar statements I hear are:

- 'I don't know how.'
- 'It's easier to let things go.'
- 'I have children.' (!)
- 'If I get organised, I won't be creative any more.'

- 'My problems are different from those of everyone else (I get more post, I have more appointments, responsibilities, etc.), so I can't get organised.'

While people may believe these excuses are true, the fact remains that people who are successful share a common secret. They know that to get ahead, they must plan, set priorities, and always follow through. In the process, they develop systems that work for them.

Their reward? Peace of mind and a gift of extra time no more looking for the missing file folder, the other sock, or a friend's telephone number. (It's frightening to imagine the hours wasted on disorganisation!)

Organisation is being able to find what you're looking for – getting things done – being in control of your life. Why spend time looking for your keys when you could be locking the door and heading out to have a good time?

With most people, I find that there comes a time when they simply have to face the fact that because of disorganisation, their lives aren't working for them: for one client things got so bad she had to move out of her apartment; another came to me because she couldn't stand having her checks bounce anymore; a third telephoned saying her desk 'looked like an archaeological dig, there were so many levels of civilisation to uncover . . .'; a fourth called after she bought a new evening dress and shoes and had her hair done for a black tie event – only to go on the wrong night. One called immediately after he had seen my name in the newspaper. I was impressed with his efficiency until he said, 'I was afraid that if I didn't call you now, I would lose the little scrap of paper I've written your number on.' The list goes on and on.

I recently met a woman who said, 'I'm so disorganised that I go to the supermarket and I forget why I'm there. I get to a meeting, and I've left the papers I needed behind; I'm always late . . . My life would be so simple if only I were organised.'

'Why do you avoid getting organised?' I asked her.

'I guess I just don't know how,' was her reply.

You've bought this book, so you must have decided that – for you – now is the time to learn how to get organised. And I've got good news for you: anybody can get organised if they want to badly enough.

Organisation is a skill that can be learned. The most difficult part is breaking those lifelong bad habits (like letting your paperwork pile up). The key to getting better organised is to start with one small step and then take others, one at a time. You may find that what you've put off for years takes only an hour to do! And once you see the benefits in one part of your life, you'll be motivated to go on.

If you implement the ideas given here, you'll be free from chaos and feel in charge of your life. Just do me one favour. Once you've started, stick with it. Getting organised is the first step; persistence and follow-through will keep you that way.

You may want to read the book straight through or go directly to the chapter that interests you most. Just keep working away, and keep *Organise Yourself!* around for easy reference. You'll find it handy to refer to time and again. Now let's get started.

PART I

Getting Control of Your Time

1

Procrastination

Are you a procrastinator? Here are some warning signs.

- Do you often wait until the last minute to start a project?
- Do you frequently send belated birthday cards?
- Do you do all your Christmas shopping on Christmas Eve?
- Do you regularly put off going to the doctor or dentist?
- Have you been meaning for ages to clean out your cupboards/drawers/kitchen/medicine cabinet?
- Do you often put off making decisions?
- Are you waiting for the 'right' time to make that dreaded phone call, confront your boss about a well-deserved pay rise, or start an exercise programme?
- Did you leave this chapter till last?

Most of us procrastinate in one area or another. Some people procrastinate about everything. It's only natural. As children, we learnt that procrastination brought a certain element of satisfaction. If we delayed a task (like cleaning our room at Mum's request), we at least gained some control over it; we had to do it, but at least we said when. That's important to a child who has so little say over many things. What's more, if we procrastinated long enough, we found sometimes that someone (good old Mum) might even do it for us – and that was worth waiting for!

As adults, procrastination generally signals some type of internal conflict. While we've made the decision to do something, there is still a part of us that holds back. Here are some of the reasons why people procrastinate:

- They feel overwhelmed. This usually happens when there is an overload of information or too many details.
- They over-estimate the time needed. They think the task is too time-consuming, that it will take for ever. A variation of this is thinking that they have for ever to finish something.
- They'd rather be doing something else. Anything seems better than what awaits them.
- They think that if they wait long enough, the 'problem' will go away. The project will be cancelled or the appointment postponed, for example.
- They want to do it perfectly. People are often apprehensive about handing in a report or finishing a project because they worry about failing on 'judgement day'. They delay until the last minute, and then, if it doesn't come up to scratch, they say, 'Oh, I would have done better if I'd had more time.'
- They don't want to assume responsibility. After all, if they never complete the project, no one will hold them responsible.
- They fear success. If they complete something and succeed, will they be able to continue to live up to that standard? How will others relate to them once they are successful?
- They say they enjoy the last-minute adrenalin rush. Often people feel that they do their best work 'under pressure'. What they fail to remember are the times when they had a terrible cold or there was a family emergency during the time they had intended to devote to the project.

Identifying your reasons for procrastinating

- First you must determine which situations generally cause you to procrastinate. Consider the following questions:
  - In what types of situation do you usually procrastinate?
  - How has it worked against you?
  - What price did you pay for the delay?

- When you procrastinated for a long time and then finally acted, what motivated you in the end? (Imminent deadline? Reward? Some outside pressure?)

■ When you find yourself procrastinating about something specific, consider the following:

- What aspect of this situation causes conflict for you? What are you avoiding?

- If you delay, what is likely to be the result?

- If the question really is *when* you will do it, and not *if*, ask yourself if you really want to pay the price of a delay.

Twenty-seven ways to stop procrastinating

■ The hardest part is getting started. Once you're in motion, it will be easier to keep going. You may well find that it isn't as bad as you expected, and once you're involved, you've overcome the highest hurdle.

■ A more realistic sense of time will help you get things done. Procrastinators often have an unrealistic sense of time; you may have the feeling that a project will take for ever or that you have 'plenty of time'. The more realistic you become, the less likely you'll be to procrastinate. To get a better sense of time, start keeping a log of how long various projects take. (Use your desk diary or your computer calendar to keep track. You can do a tally at the end of each month.) How long did you really spend making those sales calls? Only one hour? That wasn't too bad. How long did it take to pack for a family holiday? How much time did you spend doing your family budget?

■ Work with the time available to you. Sometimes people estimate that a project will take 10 or 12 hours, so they keep waiting for a day when they can devote that amount of time to it. Of course, that day never comes. Break the project down into small, manageable parts. List each step you need to take in order to complete the task. For example, if you're planning a house move, begin by researching which removal company to use. Ask friends for recommendations, and get prices from some of the companies which advertise. Keep a record of what you learn, and you'll soon be prepared to make a decision. (And note that selecting a removals firm is just one part of the very large task of moving house.)

■ Consider your 'To do' list inviolate. Once a task from the project gets written down on that list, then it shall be done.

■ Remember that even five minutes is enough time to get something done. Two phone calls or more can be completed in that time.

■ If it seems like there really is no time, carve out half an hour or so from your existing schedule. If you really want to take up jogging, try getting up half an hour earlier each day (or at weekends). If you want to do it, you'll find the time.

■ Consider the place where you work. Perhaps it's simply not convenient. One client constantly complained that she never had time to write, though she enjoyed it. When I visited her I saw why. Her computer was in one part of the house; her notes and files were in a cupboard, and her books were scattered on the floor. She then had to carry everything to a fourth location where she liked to work. Simply setting up was such a complicated procedure, it was no wonder she never wrote!

■ Clear your work area of distractions, and don't let your eyes wander.

■ You don't always have to start at the beginning. If that first step seems the hardest, start with another part of the project instead.

■ Some people like to do the worst first. If they accomplish what they dislike most, the rest of the project seems to proceed more smoothly.

■ Set small deadlines for yourself. For example, a major desk organisation schedule might include:

• purchase desktop organisers by 20 April;

• establish a Desk Workbook by 30 April;

• finish sorting through papers by 8 May.

For more information, see Chapter 10.

- Tell someone else what your deadline is. Often you will be motivated by not wanting to admit to them that you did not meet the deadline.

- Try tricking yourself: 'If I don't finish writing this proposal by 5 p.m., then I will have to cancel my plans for tonight.' Working against that sort of deadline can be quite effective!

- After each small deadline, promise yourself a reward. Perhaps it could be a new book or a tennis lesson. After the project is completed, think on a grander scale and promise yourself dinner out and a trip to the cinema, or tickets to a football match.

- Try to do things as they occur to you. The more papers you process as they arrive in the post, or the more tasks you complete as you think of them, the less opportunity you will have to procrastinate.

- Ask yourself, 'Is there a simpler way to do it?' Maybe you're making the task more difficult than it is. Do you really need to make dessert for the party from scratch or would a fruit platter do just as well?

- Ask yourself, 'What's the worst thing that will happen if I do it?' Perhaps you'll spend a beautiful Saturday afternoon indoors finishing your project, but isn't that better than worrying all day Saturday whether you'll feel like doing it on Sunday?

- Do nothing! Try sitting with the project in front of you for 15 minutes without touching it. You will probably become so frustrated that you'll dive into the project well before the 15 minutes are up.

- Listen to your moods. When you feel motivated, use that energy to get the project done. Some people use anger as a motivation to scrub the floor or clean a cupboard, and why not? It makes them feel better by burning off the excess energy caused by the anger, and they accomplish something they probably wouldn't otherwise.

- Plan an appropriate reason to be motivated. For example, if you have been procrastinating about getting your rugs and windows cleaned, invite some friends to Sunday lunch. They may not care how clean your house is, but it might be enough to motivate you to act.

■ Be opportunistic. If your father calls to say he'll be half an hour late, take those 30 minutes and make a stab at something you've put off. Or if a meeting that would have taken a full afternoon is cancelled, consider working on a special project that needs your attention. With a full afternoon, you have a longer period of time to concentrate.

■ Expect problems. The children may get ill. You may be delayed coming back from your trip. If you anticipate that you won't actually have 'all of next week' to work on something, then you may be motivated to start a little earlier.

■ If you tend to stall when you've almost finished with a project, maybe you fear being judged once you're finished. Be kind to yourself. At heart, you know it doesn't really need to be perfect.

■ If you've promised to get back to someone about a decision but haven't made up your mind yet, call and tell him you haven't made up your mind, but you will get back to him. Then at least you don't add feelings of guilt (about not getting back in touch) to your indecision.

■ Remember that you really are not the only one who can do the job well, so delegate to someone else what you would rather not do or hire someone to do it for you. You could also barter with a friend. If she'll organise your files, you can help set up her computer.

■ Make sure you use your leisure time for leisure. Most procrastinators ruin much of their free time because they are worrying about whether 'tomorrow' is really enough time to get something done. Learning to do things in advance provides the opportunity for worry-free leisure.

■ Sometimes procrastination is a decision in itself. If you don't get around to sending for the travel brochures you promised you'd send for, think again. Maybe you don't really want to go away just at the moment.

2

Managing Interruptions

- You never have the chance to take a nap, but this afternoon you're so sleepy and everyone is gone, so you decide to lie down for a few minutes . . . The phone rings.
- It's Friday afternoon, and you're just getting ready to leave work . . . An 'urgent' fax comes in, and now you're stuck doing the work the fax requires.
- Finally, you have an hour to work on that project that needs to be finished, and you've just got yourself organised to begin when . . . a colleague decides to drop in for a visit.

Does any of this sound familiar? Probably. Interruptions are very much a part of our lives.

While some interruptions can be prevented, many are inevitable, and the best you can hope for is to manage them.

Planning

Most interruptions happen because the priorities of someone else come into conflict with your plans. A colleague comes into your office and sits down to chat; your child wants you to get her more juice; your husband thinks you must know where his blue shirt is; the list goes on and on. Here are some ways to minimise these types of interruption:

- Ask friends and family not to drop in without notice.
- Group together interruptions that are within your control. If you are taking a day off from work so that some furniture can be delivered, for example, arrange for the plumber and the

television repair person to come on the same day. Narrow this block of time as much as possible by arranging everything either for the morning or the afternoon.

■ Help your family help themselves. Determine what they most frequently request from you. Food? Help in finding things? Try to arrange things so that they can do it without having to ask you. For example, healthy snack food, such as carrot sticks, and juice can be provided in such a way that a four-year-old can get it himself. If your partner has a particular weakness, such as losing things, try to establish a system so that you don't have to be the one who always works out where things are. If finding a pen always seems to be a problem, for example, stock up on so many that he or she can't possibly not find one.

■ Teach your family that a closed door or a Do Not Disturb sign means business.

■ Learn to say no. If you feel you've acted as family servant and kind neighbour once too often this weekend, and you have no private time of your own, stand your ground. A simple no will sometimes make the interruption go away.

■ Set up rewards. If you have a successful half an hour or hour with no interruptions, promise the children a treat such as playing a favourite game. For your partner, you might prepare a favourite dinner or leave a card expressing your thanks.

■ Turn on the telephone answering machine or use voice-mail when you need some quiet time. (See Chapter 3 for additional information about handling interruptions from the telephone.)

■ As a last resort, leave the house. Sometimes, investing in a babysitter – or if children aren't the problem, simply getting away – is the best way to have uninterrupted time. Go to the library, or the park in the summer, and enjoy your time there. At the office, find a quiet conference room where you can accomplish what you need.

Managing interruptions

- If someone over the age of four is interrupting you, try the following:
  - 'How can I help you?'
  - 'I'd love to hear about it, but could I come and discuss it once I've finished my project?' For children, you need to speak of time in relation to something they understand. You might say, 'Can I come and discuss it once you've listened to both sides of your tape?'
- Don't prolong a conversation or do anything to extend an interruption. Once you've been interrupted, it's tempting to stop what you're doing, but remember that this is the time you intended to devote to something specific (whether it was personal time or paying your bills), so make sure that you get straight back to it.
- Plan for the fact that there will be interruptions. If the phone is your main interrupter, there will be times when you don't have your answering machine turned on, so keep small projects near the phone to work on during a conversation. A long cord on a phone in the kitchen lets you dice food, fix snacks, or prepare lunch while talking. Make use of that time.

Don't be your own interrupter

- Don't use interruptions as an excuse to avoid your work.
- Don't make the mistake of initiating phone calls or visits to break the peace.
- Don't encourage unnecessary personal telephone calls from family and friends.
- Don't start another project before you finish the first one.
- Don't procrastinate. Once you have the time, use it!

3

The Telephone

How many times have you really gained momentum on a task only to be interrupted by a telephone call you really didn't want to take?

How often have you been stuck on the telephone, trying to get off, but somehow unable to end the conversation?

And what about the times you've been put on hold for what seems like an eternity – especially when *they've* phoned *you*!

Or how many times have you phoned someone only to forget one of the reasons why you called?

The telephone is a great invention and can be a terrific convenience and time-saver. But few people realise that they don't have to permit it to rule the household or workplace by allowing callers to interrupt meals, delay departures, waste their time with needlessly long calls, and otherwise cause inconvenience. We can all learn to control the telephone so it doesn't control us.

Establishing a telephone centre

First, you need to organise the area around your telephone so that you can make and receive calls efficiently.

- A pad and pen should be kept by every telephone in the house, and conveniently located near office phones, too. Keep an extra pad near by at all times so that you can re-stock easily. If your pens tend to 'wander', buy a pen on a cord and attach it to the telephone.

- Keep your calendar or diary, telephone directories and code book, and a list of personal telephone numbers close to the phone that you use most frequently.

Before you place a call

Perhaps the easiest telephone habits to alter concern your outgoing calls; changing your habits can result in substantial time-saving.

- Establish a 'telephone time', during which you make all necessary calls. By making all the calls at one sitting, rather than throughout the day, you are more likely to stay with the task at hand rather than to digress and have a chat with someone.

- To avoid having to call someone more than once, make notes about what you need to discuss. If you need to make just a few calls, with only a point or two to be discussed with each person, you can easily make your notes on your calendar. However, if you're doing lots of phoning (on a regular basis or even just on one day), use your telephone pad for some pre-planning. On the top line of the page note the person's name, telephone number, and the date. Beneath that, note the points that need to be discussed. As you talk, you should write down any significant information from the conversation. A typical page might look like this:

JACK'S RENT A CAR
0181-222 2222

What is your daily rate?

How many free miles?

Where can the car be picked up and returned?

Record the replies on the bottom and then compare the information with other car rental services you are calling.

- When your calls are completed, transfer important information, such as the date you need to follow up with someone, to your calendar or diary, or to your files (for example, answers from your accountant regarding your taxes to your tax file). Then throw away the paper.

- As you dial, concentrate on the call you are making and what you need to discuss. When phoning several people at one sitting, there is a tendency to let your mind drift and forget whom you've called.

- Get to the point of your call quickly and stick to it.
- Take care of business before pleasure. If you need to discuss financial matters with your broker, make sure all business is taken care of before having a social chat.
- Don't let the person babble. If their reply begins to wander, don't hesitate to bring them back to the conversation with a polite but firm, 'Do you have that information or could you suggest someone else for me to call?'

Ending conversations

Sometimes getting off the phone can be an art in itself. Certain people – you know the type – ignore all the subtle signals you give; they must keep talking. Here are some tips on how to free yourself more quickly:

- Warn them in advance that your time is limited: 'It sounds interesting, but I've got to leave here in five minutes. Can you tell me about it briefly?'
- Try inserting 'before we hang up' as a mental warning to the other person that the call will end soon.
- At home, keep a kitchen timer near each phone. When you want to get off, set it so that the bell rings, and you can announce, 'Well, I have to go. I've got to take something out of the oven.'
- At the office, try pretending someone has arrived for a meeting, so that you've got to get off the phone.
- For the person who calls frequently, you'll soon run out of contrived exit lines. Try being straight with them: 'I really can't spend a lot of time on the telephone. Let's make plans to meet for lunch instead.'

If you don't know where the time goes . . .

- Telephone conversations last longer than you think. Time them by keeping a clock by the phone. One client limits all calls – not just those that are long-distance – to no longer than five minutes and uses a timer to remind himself.

- If you don t really know why the phone is taking up so much of your time, try logging your calls. Keep a sheet of paper near each phone and list the following: the time of the call, the name of the person with whom you spoke, who originated the call, what you were doing when the call interrupted, and the subject and length of the call.

Time	Person	Originator	Pre-call activity	Subject	Length

A quick scan of the sheet after a week or so will tell you how your telephone time is spent. Then you can determine how to eliminate or shorten certain calls. You may find that you've been taking calls throughout the day when what you really needed was a block of uninterrupted time. Or there may be one person who calls you almost every morning (when you're especially busy) just to pass the time. You can solve the problem by suggesting a better time to talk.

New telephones that extend your range

Like it or not, today telephones can go with you almost anywhere. Though there may be days when you wish you could go back to a time before telephones, for the majority of people these new inventions make life more convenient and save time:

- The cordless phone (distinct from a cellular phone because it still has to be within 100 feet or so of a 'home base') is perfect for use at home. Because you aren't tethered by a cord, you can sit on your porch and make a telephone call, or you can take the phone with you while you do some tidying up around the house.

- The cellular or mobile phone was initially for use in the car, but today it is increasingly common to see them being used wherever you go. Mobile phones are helpful in an emergency: they keep you in constant touch with family, friends, and colleagues, and enable you to save time by making some calls when you're stuck in traffic. (Remember to turn it off, though, when you to go your child's school concert. There are some things that really shouldn't be interrupted.)

Consider a beeper

Beepers aren't just for doctors any more. Today they are used in a wide range of businesses, as well as by people such as expectant fathers who want to be contactable at the critical moment, and by teenagers whose parents want to be able to reach them at certain times (usually late at night).

Beepers are now much more sophisticated than the one-way pagers they were designed to be. Today you can buy a two-way model that offers the possibility of relaying short messages. Not only will users receive a phone number and a simple text message, but they'll also be able to reply. Because beepers of the future will need keyboards to send lengthy messages, it is expected that most two-way systems will use the new palmtop computers as their basic tool. (You can read more about these in Chapter 9.)

Telephone company add-ons that make sense

Telephone companies have developed a number of additional services that can make your life easier. The following are some of the ones you might like to know about (some home phone systems now have these features built into the unit):

- 'Caller identification' provides you with a screen display of the number of the telephone from which the call is originating. This allows you to choose whether to pick up right away or let it ring, and reduces the risk of nuisance calls.

- 'Call waiting' beeps you when you re on the telephone and another call is coming through – it's almost as good as having a second line. This way, you no longer need to keep the line free if you're expecting another call. If you have children in the house, you may need to set rules on whose call takes priority when 'call waiting' beeps.

- 'Call forwarding' transfers an incoming call to whatever number you specify. You can forward calls to your holiday home or send them through to your voice-mail system if you're away and can't be reached.

- When the person you want to call is engaged, press 5 to use the 'call back' facility. This keeps calling the chosen number and calls you back when the line becomes free. A further facility allows you to identify missed callers by keying in 1471; you can then dial the number of the last person to call you by pressing 3.

Special telephone features that save time

Today's programmable telephones have added features that would amaze and thrill telephone inventor Alexander Graham Bell. When you shop for a system, look for the following:

- Speed dialling. Many systems can store your frequently called or most useful numbers, such as the local police station, your mother, and your best client.

- Speaker phone. For hands-free calling or for waiting while on hold, a speaker phone offers great convenience. Punch the 'speaker' button, and you're free to do what you need to do.

- Automatic redial. If the number you're calling is busy, simply push 'redial' on your telephone. The system will let you know when it's got through.

- Mute button. This is a vital addition to any phone being used in a home office. When the dog barks or the baby cries during a business call, just press 'mute' to cover up the sounds.

- Conference calling. If you have more than one telephone line, this feature allows you to set up three-way calls so that you can have 'meetings' over the phone, and speak to more than one relative or friend at the same time.

Answering machines and voice-mail

Answering machines are familiar to most people these days, but in the work environment they are increasingly being replaced by voice-mail systems. Today, when the person you're trying to contact isn't in the office, chances are you'll be dealt with by a voice-mail message instead of a secretary.

The money spent on an answering machine or a voice-mail system is well worth the investment. Here's why:

- The machine or system can receive calls while you're not there, meaning that you get all the information you need, such as news of cancelled appointments and changed meetings.

- With voice-mail, you can send the same message to several people within a company; messages can be stored and retrieved selectively; callers can leave messages 24 hours a day; and you can add beeper capabilities if you're in a business where you may need to be reached instantly.

- Callers are now so accustomed to voice-mail and answering machines and many will leave a long precise message. A system with unlimited time for recording incoming messages can serve you and your callers as a 'secretary'. A detailed message can save both parties extra phoning. (A business associate of mine often phones people hoping to get their machine so she can leave one efficient message and be done with it.)

- Get in the habit of keeping your outgoing messages current; this is particularly helpful with a business voice-mail system. If you're out of the office for a few days, your message can tell callers that so they know they may not hear from you right away.

- Would you like callers to leave an 'organised message' instead of a rambling one? Tell them that on your greeting. I do, and it works!

- You can use the machine to screen calls. If you're working on a project or taking a break, you can leave the machine on to monitor who is calling. If it's urgent, you can answer it. If it's not, you can call them back later, at *your* convenience.

- If you have an assistant who screens your voice-mail, ask for a log of all calls to be kept. Lengthy or detailed messages should be 'archived' so that you can listen to them yourself.

- Receiving a call when you're on your way out can cause annoying delays. One solution is to turn on your machine or voice-mail system about 15 minutes before you need to leave. If you're on your way to an appointment, call and confirm in advance; this will keep you from missing a possible cancellation call.

Additional ways to control your calls

- Ask someone else to answer your phone for you at certain times. You can return the favour by doing the same for him or her.
- Turn off your home phone or unplug it when you don't want to be disturbed, such as at meal-times.

Other telephone tips

- When you have many incoming and outgoing calls, keep a list of calls to make and a list of expected returns.
- Avoid 'telephone tag'. When you leave a message for someone to call you, give a time when you'll be available, and when it will be convenient, to receive the call.
- When leaving messages, be specific and clear, providing as much information as possible, so you can eliminate extra phoning later.
- Ask others when it's a good time to call them. If you haven't been able to reach them during your 'telephone time', you'll need some indication as to when they might be available.
- Return telephone calls. You'll increase your credibility if you do.
- If someone takes messages for you, brief him to ensure he gets the correct information by repeating back the caller's name and number.
- Have a long cord on your telephone, or consider buying a cordless phone. If you need something from your files, you can retrieve it while still talking, and you will also be able to keep track of your family's whereabouts.
- If you find yourself disturbed by someone else's fax machine repeatedly calling your number by mistake, as it may be

programmed to do, phone the operator, who can interrupt the line and prevent the erroneous fax calls.

The next time you think: 'I can't believe how much time I've wasted on the phone!' re-read this chapter and see if there isn't a way to accomplish what you need to do in less time.

4

Getting Out of the House on Time

One day, a colleague and I were to attend a meeting together; about an hour before we were scheduled to be there, I had a frantic phone call from him. He'd been running late that morning and had forgotten all the papers for the meeting as well as his diary, where he had written the address of where we were to meet. It was too late to go back, so he had phoned me for the address and we had to do without the papers that day.

Another friend forgets things but remembers them just before she actually drives away from home. She frequently has to rush back into the house for her child's lunch, her diary, or the dry cleaning she wants to drop off that day, and this, of course, often makes her late.

A common reason people run late is because they practise 'at-the-door' planning. They don't consider what they need for the day until they are on the point of leaving; or they get everything organised, but leave it in the kitchen or bedroom where it is all too easily forgotten when they're running out of the front door. Needless to say, this type of leave-taking is almost always a bad start to the day. Here's how to smooth out your departure.

Do ahead of time

- Lay out your clothes the night before; this is quickly and easily done if your cupboards are well organised. Don't hang up anything if it needs to be cleaned, mended or ironed. If necessary, shoes should be shined before being returned to the closet.

- To avoid a last-minute key hunt, establish a place where keys are always kept.
- Set the breakfast table.
- Pack your handbag or briefcase and leave it in a convenient spot by the place where you keep your coat.
- Think in advance about what you need to do in the morning. Work out how many minutes each task will take, and add travel time and an additional 15 to 20 minutes for traffic and 'surprises'. This will allow you to plan exactly how long you need to get out of the house on time.
- For an especially early departure (or for those who need extra help in the morning), leave out – and group together – coat, scarf, gloves, hat, purse, briefcase, keys, transportation money, and anything else you need for a quick exit.

Set the morning routine

- Make your bed as soon as you get up.
- Use an answering machine to screen morning calls so you don't get bogged down by a conversation that could be held later in the day.
- To avoid congestion in the bathroom, schedule different shower times for family members. Bathing or showering in the evening can also reduce friction in the morning.
- Stay with the task you start. Don't hop from room to room as you get ready. As you leave each room, tidy up as you go, and take items such as your coffee cup with you.
- Call to confirm any appointments before you leave home and double check that the person you are seeing is running on time. Never assume that other people are as organised as you are.
- If time is really tight, ask yourself: 'OK, what must be done now to get me out the door, and what can wait?' (You must get dressed; the dishes can wait.) Just keep asking yourself the same question until you're out of the door.

Especially for parents

- Have contingency plans in case one of your school-age children is ill or if the baby-sitter is late or doesn't turn up at all.
- The night before:
  - Lay out children's clothing.
  - Make lunches.
  - Re-pack the baby's nappy bag, if needed.
- In the morning, get up and be dressed first so you can sort out the children's more easily.
- Allow extra time for last-minute occurrences.

For the chronically late

I'm sure you've heard people jokingly say, 'He's always late; he'd be late to his own wedding.' Well, I've got a sister like that, and she was late to her own wedding! She did her make-up at home but wanted to put on her dress at the place where the wedding was being held; because she was running so late all the guests saw the bride arrive, beautifully made up, but wearing jeans.

If you're like my sister, here are some tips that might help out:

- Put yourself on a tight and consistent schedule. Routines soon become second nature and make it easier to get moving and get things done.
- Have a clock in every room, including the bathroom.
- Set the clocks a few minutes ahead.
- In your diary, mark your appointments a little earlier than they really are.
- Set a kitchen timer for 15-minute time slots. The bell will remind you how much time has passed.
- Ask a friend to call to get you moving or even stop to pick you up.

5

Preserving Personal Time

When I ask people about their 'personal time', they often laugh and say, 'Personal time? You must be joking!'

There's no doubt about it. In today's fast-paced society, with so many things to do and so many things to attract our attention, it's very difficult to set aside time for ourselves. Some people spend their personal time taking a relaxing jog in the morning when they can let their minds drift. Some read a good book. Others think the best thing in the world is having time to call an old friend.

However you choose to spend such time, you've got to work to preserve it. Here are some tips.

Finding the time

- The first thing you need to do is decide how you can best provide for some personal time. Some people like to schedule it – a workaholic might reserve Sunday afternoons for herself; a mother might schedule a regular babysitter once a week so that she can have time off. One couple I know has standing appointments with a sitter for every Thursday and Saturday night so they know they'll have time off together. Others find it satisfactory to take time as needed. When they are really feeling overwhelmed, then they work to carve out time for themselves.

- Some people steal their personal time from their 'sleeping time' by getting up a half-hour or an hour earlier. (Set your alarm earlier by ten-minute increments to adjust gradually to the new wake-up time.)

- You can also borrow personal time from 'waiting time' while in your doctor's office, or during a bus or train ride; or you can use the time gained from a cancelled appointment.

- If you have children, make it clear you need time on your own. If you've organised a half-hour activity for them while you have a break, explain that this is *your* time. Or explain that you'll play or talk with them when their game or TV show is over.

- To have personal time you must guard your right to it, but sometimes you'll need to be creative. With my family's hectic schedule, I now find time to exercise before the household gets up. It's worth it to me to find this time by working around the family's schedule.

- Make a definite decision as to how you want to spend your personal time, or it will simply slip away from you. Do you want to spend it alone? With the family? With friends? And what sort of activity would you like to do?

Make a firm resolve to protect that time, just as you would guard a commitment you made in any other part of your life.

6

How to Use a Kitchen Timer to Manage Time

A simple kitchen timer can prove invaluable as a reminder or as an aid in managing small blocks of time. Buy a portable timer so you can use it in various parts of the house.

Here are 15 ways to use a kitchen timer:

- As a way to time (and limit) your morning shower. Aim for stay in no longer than three minutes.

- As a reminder to make a telephone call.

- As a reminder to try a call again when the phone was engaged the first time.

- To limit telephone conversations that tend to get lengthy; set the timer for five minutes.

- As an incentive to start something. If you've been procrastinating on a project, set your timer for 10 minutes and promise to work that long on what you don't want to do. Chances are you'll no longer feel blocked by the undertaking, but if you do, use the 10-minute system again the next day until you're comfortable with the project or until you've finished it.

- As a way to start exercising: 'I'll exercise for just 15 minutes.'

- As a way to motivate yourself to organise your desk: 'I'll spend just 10 minutes sorting papers.'

- Play 'beat the clock' to get the chores done around the house: 'I bet I can clean all the mirrors and windows in less than 15 minutes.'

- When working in blocks of time (such as spending half an hour setting up a library for your books). Stop when the timer goes off.

- As a reminder to turn off the stove, the sprinkler, and so on.

- To tell you when it is time for something, for example, a special television programme or a favourite radio show.

- As a way to time a discussion or argument. Each person gets three minutes to present his side of the case.

- To free you from worrying about time. If you come home and have only 45 minutes until you must leave again, set the timer rather than watching the clock. It frees you to focus on something else while guaranteeing that you'll know when it's time to go out again.

- As a way to help a small child cope with waiting time. If a youngster wants your attention when you can't give it, set the timer for when you'll have finished your task. Tell the child to play until the bell goes off and then you'll read her a story.

- As a way to time 'turns'. When two toddlers get into an unresolvable argument over whose turn it is to play with a certain toy, try giving each of them five minutes with it. The ringing bell signals that the turn is over.

PART II

Paperwork

7

Books

Most people like to have books around, but the book collection of one of my clients was enormous. Her walls were covered with books; she used books as end tables, and to support a missing leg of a bed; books lurked in every nook and cranny of her house. She had to create aisles between the piles of books so that she could move from room to room. It felt as though part of the British Library was housed in her sitting room.

Whatever the size of our book collection, most of us have occasion to refer back to a book we read a few years ago – and then can't locate it. We wonder, 'Did I throw it out? Did I lend it to someone? Did I put it away in a box? Or is it still here somewhere on my shelves?'

Here's a way to establish a logical system for your home library so that you'll be able to find any book when you need it.

To establish a system

- Have on hand a few empty cardboard boxes for books you may want to donate to charity or put away in an attic or cellar. Get your step-ladder so you'll be able to reach high shelves.

- If you have a reasonable number of books, gather them together to make an inventory.

- If you have a large collection with books in several rooms, tackle the project on room by room. Work in blocks of time: do the study on Monday, the bedroom on Tuesday, and so on.

- Divide books into useful categories, such as travel, baby care, and so on, to suit your collection.

- As you categorise, look out for books that could be donated to charity, or to your local hospital, library or school. You might also try selling some to places that buy old or used books.

- Next, put away in boxes those books that you want to save but don't need to access (those you're saving for your children, and those you don't expect to refer to). Label the boxes clearly and store them in the attic, the cellar, or at the back of a cupboard.

- Make an inventory of the books you want to keep and have accessible. Do you have adequate shelf space for them? Perhaps you can build shelves in the kitchen for cookery books, or you may want to buy a free-standing bookcase for the sitting room. Whether buying or building, keep in mind that it's helpful to be able to adjust the height between the shelves.

- As much as possible, keep your books where you will be using them. Cookery books in the kitchen, children's books in the children's rooms, reference books near your desk, and so on.

- Select specific shelves where certain books will be stored. Frequently used books should be within easy reach.

- After you have decided where each book category will go, organise the books according to sub-category. For example, cookery books might best be sorted by type of cooking – French, vegetarian, and so on. History books might best be arranged by period.

- Alphabetise within each sub-division either by title or author, depending on which you remember first about a book.

- When putting the books away, consider placing some books horizontally; this can provide variation in the look of the bookcase and also make titles easier to read.

- If you have so many books that some must be kept out of reach on high shelves, in cupboards or in double rows, consider a catalogue system. Write the book's title, author and subject, and its location, on an index card, and keep the cards in a file card box with sub-divider cards labelled according to subject category. You can then organise each category alphabetically by title or author. This cataloguing could also be done on your computer.

Other tips

- If people borrow books from you, create a system so that you'll know where your books are. Use a page in your Desk Workbook (see Chapter 10) to record the book's title, the date it was borrowed, the borrower's name, when he or she plans to return it, and his or her telephone number.

- If you're on the verge of having an unmanageable collection like the client I described earlier, consider using the public library rather than buying more books. She would have saved herself a lot of space if she had made a few trips there herself!

8

Diaries

One year in early January I had dinner with a friend who had made a New Year's resolution to reform and get organised. As we talked, she started telling me that her new diary system would be the key to her organisation, and she proudly began pulling things from a huge bag she was carrying. Out came a 'month-at-a-glance' diary, a daily planner for personal appointments, another diary for work only, and a large hard-back notebook for jotting down inspirations. I had to tell her I didn't think this system would ever get her organised – it was just a lot of extra baggage to carry around! As you'll see, she would have been better off had she purchased just one diary. With the right one, she could have kept track of everything.

Diaries come in all shapes and sizes. Some have lovely artwork or literary quotations, while others are more businesslike. Now you can also buy electronic diaries or computer programs that will do the job for you.

Regardless of the kind of diary you use, it must be a convenient one, and you should feel comfortable with it. A diary used regularly and effectively can become an important tool in a well-organised life.

- Use only one daily diary. (A family will also want a wall diary in the kitchen to keep track of family members' whereabouts.) The 'single daily diary' rule is vital, yet some people think they can't live without two or three. The problem with having more than one diary is that you may forget to transfer information from one place to another. For example, keeping one appointment diary at home and another at the office is a logical but unwise practice. One businesswoman I know switched to a one-diary system the morning she arrived at a restaurant for a meeting only to discover two clients awaited her – she had set up two breakfast appointments for the same day!

■ Choose the type of diary you feel most comfortable with. You may like the 'week-at-a-glance' layout, or to have a page or two devoted to each day, or you may be ready to go electronic. In choosing, keep in mind that a good diary should be large enough to provide space to record appointments and activities, to make notes (such as questions to ask at your next appointment), and to keep a list of errands and projects to accomplish that day. It should also be small enough to carry with you at all times.

A good diary might also include:

- a telephone directory (for frequently called numbers);
- an expense record;
- extra pages for notes (handy for jotting down ideas while you're on the go).

■ Record everything. Don't trust yourself (or clutter your mind) with having to remember that dinner date with your neighbours next Tuesday. Even a regular Friday afternoon squash game should be noted so that when you glance at Friday, you have a picture of what the day holds for you. If appointments are not written down, you may unintentionally forget about one of them.

■ When using your diary to record an appointment, write down the address, telephone number and directions in the space next to the appointment. The more information of this type you write down, the better your diary will serve as a helpful record if you need to go back and check something later on in the year.

■ Always review your activities at least one week in advance so you know what is scheduled and can make any changes if you need to.

■ At the office, provide a printout of the day's or week's appointments so that colleagues know your whereabouts. If you have a secretary who keeps your diary, he or she should leave a photocopy for you. (See below for additional ideas on scheduling using a computerised diary.)

■ Daily, or every few days, review plans with the person you live with, especially when you both carry a diary. This way, each of you will know when the other will be late coming home, or will be going away, and you can also be aware of and note places where you are going together.

The family wall diary

■ Purchase a large calendar to hang in a central place near a telephone. In most homes this is the kitchen.

■ Assign each family member a colour and write down each one's activities as and when they are organised. Choose a colour for joint family activities too, and make sure they also appear on the diary.

■ When children are old enough to start taking responsibility for their own plans, it's time for them to write them down on their own. Parents should write down plans they make that affect the children, such as 'Sunday dinner at Grandma's' or 'Mum late home'. Children should record all their plans on the diary; this way, if you arrive home one afternoon and find your child isn't there yet, you can quickly check to see where he or she is. Also write down regular appointments such as Sunday school or gym class.

■ Make a habit of checking the wall diary daily to see if there is information there that you need to add to your personal diary. You don't want to schedule a meeting at the time you promised to pick up your daughter and her friends at the ice rink.

Computer diaries

Diary software for computers usually combines an appointment book, address book, 'To do' lists and space for notes. They offer terrific opportunities for organisational improvement.

- Re-scheduling can be accomplished with a few key strokes; all details pertaining to the appointment, including directions on how to get there, can be moved from Tuesday to Thursday in one go.

- The diary informs you of your availability at a glance. If you need to know if you have any free time next week, a click of the mouse will instantly provide you with the entire week's schedule.

- Dual scheduling is easy, with bosses and secretaries able to input into the same system, and therefore remain co-ordinated and up-to-date. Group scheduling, such as a departmental meeting, can also be accomplished via networked computers. You choose how much of your diary you want to make available for 'public' scheduling. The rest can be kept private.

- Regular appointments can be set to appear automatically.

- Your 'To do' list can carry over from day to day until all tasks are complete.

- Search capabilities are a part of the package. Your computer can, for example, help you find the last time you went to your optician's.

- If you have a modem, some systems feature auto-dial and auto-fax features. To fax a report to a colleague, you can look up the person's fax number in your online address book, highlight the report, and with a click on the 'fax' icon, the report will be on its way.

- 'Contact manager' versions of these diary systems provide space to log phone calls and take notes on meetings. The next time you're in touch with a particular colleague or client, you can pull up the information and pick up right where you left off.

There are a couple of drawbacks to having your diary on computer. If your computer is turned on for only a couple of hours a day, you may find that it's inconvenient to enter dates or check your address book. This can be partially overcome by working from a printout of your schedule or list of contacts when you're away from your computer, but you should keep it in mind if you're considering a switch. I know someone who loved the organisational aspects of having his diary on computer, but finally went back to a paper-based diary system after a couple of years. He said, 'I was in and out of the office so much each day that even with the information on my laptop, I just found paper was more convenient for me.'

Electronic organisers or personal digital assistants

Formerly considered just an executive toy, electronic organisers are today used by a wide range of people. The personal information manager is a hand-held electronic device designed to keep phone numbers, addresses and appointments, but these systems are generally limited in capacity because they do not interface with a computer.

More advanced is the 'personal digital assistant'. It operates much like a personal computer, and it can be connected to a fax machine or to an online service, or linked to your computer for information exchange. Palmtop computers function like organisers, keeping phone numbers and appointments, but they often include word processing and spreadsheet capabilities and sometimes wireless faxing and data reception.

If you decide some type of electronic organiser is for you, keep the following in mind as you shop for a specific model:

- Is it a convenient size and not too heavy? You want it to feel portable.

- Does it require warm-up time, and if so, is the wait a reasonable one? If someone wants to book an appointment, you don't want to have to wait long to be able to access your diary.

- How is the data entered? By keyboard? By pen on to the screen? If there is a keyboard, is it comfortable? If you are a touch typist or have large hands, some of the keyboards may feel too small. If it's a pen-based system, test to see if the organiser can decipher your handwriting.

- Compare screens. Make sure the one you select is easy to read. Those that feature backlighting tend to be more versatile.

- Ask about memory capacity, and make sure the model you're considering has the capacity for adding extra memory if you think you might need it.

- Is there a rechargeable battery pack available? Most burn through batteries quickly, so it's helpful to be able to charge a battery pack at night.
- Is there any risk of losing the information? You might want a device that connects to your computer so that you can back it up on a regular basis.
- Does it provide ready access to your phone directory, diary and 'To do' list? Do you like the format of each of these items?
- Ask if there other software available, such as a thesaurus, a dictionary, time and expense records, a foreign-language translator, city guides, financial planning programs and games.

Keep an eye on these hand-held gadgets. The technology is changing rapidly, and soon most of them will have all the capabilities of a desktop computer. A single command from this tiny instrument will send a wireless fax about Friday's 3 p.m. meeting, note the date in your diary, and add 'prepare for meeting' to your 'To do' list, all at the same time.

In the long run, this invention will be hard to resist.

9

The Family Computer

If your family is not yet computer-literate, you've probably been thinking about becoming so, as more and more of your friends talk about the benefits of computerisation. Now is a good time to get involved, and find out how a home computer can be a convenient time-saver.

Here are some of the points to keep in mind as you enter the fray – or expand your reach – during the computer age.

Buying a family computer

- If you're buying a new computer, get the most up-to-date model you can afford. Technology is developing so rapidly you will probably find that the latest equipment does everything you want it to, and more.

- Make sure your computer comes with a warranty. Many companies will offer three years warranty, with one year on-site service. Problems often occur within the first few months after delivery.

- Some modern computers come with a CD drive and a built-in modem. It is extremely likely that you will use both these features, so don't try to save a few pounds by buying a model without them.

- A scanner can turn pictures and text into electronic files for use on your computer. They are not very expensive at the moment, and they may soon even become an integral part of the home computer.

- Invest in anti-virus software, or download a program from an online service. The risk of getting a virus on a home machine is low, but if it should happen, it can be disasterous.

- Send off the registration card that comes with any computer program you buy so the company can notify you about updates.
- Ask at the place where you buy your computer for the name and number of someone who knows computers inside-out, who you can hire on an hourly basis to help you set up your system or learn something new. Don't be surprised or put off if this person turns out to be 19 years old, wearing a baseball cap and trainers.

Becoming computer-literate

- Take a course.
- Go to a bookshop or to a computer store and have a look through the computer books that cover the programs you're using. Many are now written with the most computer-phobic reader in mind, and are easy to understand and useful. Ask shop staff for recommendations, too.
- Subscribe to the computer magazine which best meets your needs.
- Whenever you invest in new software or add a feature to your computer, set aside time to become familiar with it, and make sure you read the operating instructions! Many programs come with tutorials that provide some basic exposure to the system. If you're still stuck, an hour with a tutor can get you up and running.
- If children will be using your computer, look at buying some software that prohibits them from entering your files. There are several that give children access to their own material, but allow only adult password-holders to go to information such as family finances.

Backing up is vital

- Make sure you have a good back-up system that is easy to use. If you fail to back up your files correctly, you may not have a problem for years, but a breakdown can happen, and you may suffer the devastation of losing years' worth of data.

- Most home computers need to be backed up once a month, so establish a schedule and note it in your diary. You might make it one of the things you do on the first day of the month, for example. If you use your computer frequently, you may want to back up weekly, or whenever you've entered a quantity of information.

- Computers used for work should have three levels of back-up: monthly, weekly, and daily (the daily back-up can be selective).

- If you're working on something extremely important, make two back-up copies. Store one in the desk where you've been working. Take the other one with you. If you're at the office, take it home; if you're at home, take it to the office.

Now for the fun

Here are just some of the features and capabilities of your computer which will make your life easier and more fun.

- Address book. Access information on friends, customers and colleagues at the touch of a computer key.

- Diary software. Your life at a glance. (See Chapter 8.)

- Graphic design. Now you'll write the invitation and design it, too.

- Home design. New software lets you design anything from a complete house to a decorating scheme.

- Household information. Enter anything – from an instruction sheet for a babysitter to a checklist for closing up the house when you're going to be away – and alter it as many times as you like.

- Kitchen know-how. Cookery books on computer offer the benefits of a search function. If you're looking for a chicken and oregano recipe and can't remember what it's called, the computer will find it for you.

- Legal needs. There are programs on making a will as well as programs that give you standard wording for leases, and official letters.

- Mailing lists. This type of software is a godsend if, for example, your latest volunteer job involves sending out mailings.
- Money management. Many software programs give you instant access to your finances. (See Chapters 15 and 16.)
- Photo storage. At last, you can get those photos out of the shoebox and keep them on the computer. You'll need a scanner, and then you can drop them in to personalised documents, calendars, newsletters, invitations or brochures. Or forget the printing process entirely and send photographs over the Internet to friends and relatives.
- CVs. Avoid endless typing, and make your CV look really good.
- Travel. Route-planning software can become your driving guide, working out how best you can get from A to B, and telling you what there is to see on the way.

Address books on computer

In order to be well organised, you may find that it's worth investing the time to transfer your address book to your computer. Everyone today seems to have so many ways of being contacted – home address, work address, e-mail address; office, home and mobile phone numbers; fax number – that it's very hard to find a way to keep a traditional book or system up to date.

- Computerised address books allow you to sort people's names alphabetically, geographically or by category. You may want to locate all your friends who live in Scotland, or you may be looking for the telephone number of a restaurant in Glasgow that you used to frequent regularly – ask the right questions and the computer will find the information for you.
- Print out your computer address book and keep it in a loose-leaf binder. This gives you easy access to the information even when your computer isn't on. Remember to up-date the hard copy when you enter new information by printing out a new page.
- Entering all the information into the computer is a big task, so do it in chunks, say, ten names per day. This should only take

about 10 minutes, and over a period of a few weeks you'll have
completed the entire job.

- Once your address book is complete, get in the habit of up-
dating it regularly. As soon as you receive a change of address
card, put the information in your computer. This is the key to an
up-to-date, efficient system.

Reaching the world beyond

If you have a modem (a telephone link-up that connects your computer
to a vast network) for your computer, the world is at your fingertips.
You can send and receive electronic mail, transfer money from one bank
account to another, book air tickets, use it for library research, and
spend time chatting on a 'party line'. The possibilities are far-reaching.

- If your computer does not already have a modem, invest in a
high-speed one. Book your computer 'wizard' to hook it up. If
you don't know what you're doing, you'll waste a lot of time.

- Consider having an additional phone line put in. If you've got a
fax, you could combine the two. Using one line for the
telephone, fax and modem could be frustrating.

- Investigate online services, and talk to friends and computer
dealers about software that connects you directly to the Internet.
You may decide that Internet access (for which you have to pay a
fee) through an ISP (Internet service provider) is the most
convenient; or you may opt for some of the conveniences and
features of the online services. The online services are user-
friendly and offer attractions such as 'chat rooms' and a wide
variety of research material and files that are easy to access.

- If you're using an online service, it can become expensive. You
can buy an offline reader or navigator program that lets you
more efficiently capture your mail, news and messages from your
favorite forum. It can decrease your online time considerably by
letting you download and respond to e-mail and forum messages
offline.

- If you have children, find out about the parental control features
that are available; these let your children enjoy the wonders of

interactive exploration without being exposed to unsuitable material.

If you are considering a laptop

As laptop computers (or 'notebooks') have become more functional, they've become more popular. There are dozens to choose from, so take time to select the one that best suits your family's needs.

Should you buy a laptop instead of a regular computer? Not if you have the space and don't need the portability. Desktop computers are still cheaper and easier to use, but you can't take them with you. That's when you want the laptop.

- Laptops are now about the size of a pack of photocopying paper and weigh six or seven pounds (about 3kg); some of the more expensive ones weigh even less.

- Laptop computers vary enormously in price; more speed and more hard disk space mean more money.

- Compare screens when you shop. A larger screen can have up to 60 per cent more viewing area.

- Check the 'pointing stick' or thumb pad that replaces the desktop mouse. Is it comfortable? Easy to use?

- Make sure that the laptop computer you buy has built-in connectors so that the computer can be hooked up to a printer and other peripherals. This is becoming standard, but you ought to check before you buy.

- Ask which software is already installed on the models you're considering.

- Although some computer manufacturers claim that their laptops are pretty tough, you will need to treat your new computer with respect. They are not designed to withstand being dropped or being used as a portable seat!

10

Desk Organisation

For many people, their desks are where they live for most of the day. And many of these environments are an overwhelming disaster. I'm often taken on to be a 'desk doctor', and I can't tell you the number of times I've walked in and seen an unbelievably messy desk, yet the client assures me that he or she has 'cleaned up' specially for my arrival. Referring to the magazine makeovers where ordinary people are transformed into top models, one reporter whom I visited told me, 'My desk looks like a "before" and I want it to look like an "after".' She wanted her 'hopeless mess' to become a model of efficiency. With dedication, it can be done, and that's what we'll work toward in this chapter.

I find that most of my clients' problems generally fall into one of three categories.

- Poor space planning. They have to keep jumping up and down to get the items they need.

- Poor work habits. Each day a few more papers become permanent residents of the 'To do' pile.

- Indecision. They have no idea what to do with the piles of paper on their desks.

Here are some ways to get your desk under control.

General planning

- Whether you spend one hour or eight hours at your desk every day, careful thought should go into how you use it. Make it functional!

- At home, try to establish a place that is solely for paperwork (see the building suggestions on pages 47–8). Working at the kitchen table may give you lots of space, but you don't want to have to clear your work away whenever it's time to eat.

■ It's preferable to have a desk of your own rather than sharing.

■ Know your work habits. If you like to spread out material as you work, provide yourself with enough space, such as a large desk surface or a long countertop.

■ A good chair is as important as a functional desk. Invest in one that is right for you. A chair on wheels is particularly handy.

Buying a desk

■ Shop for a desk with enough surface space so you can spread out your materials.

■ Files and supplies should be easily accessible. Some desks have shelves, filing drawers or cupboard space built into them.

■ Sit at the desk in a chair similar to the one you'll be using. The desk should feel comfortable to you, with ample room underneath for your legs.

■ I prefer desks that are wider than they are deep. Deep desks allow you to push piles of paper into the far corner, making it too easy for things to get lost.

Building new desk space

■ A practical, inexpensive desk can be made by placing a laminated board across two filing cabinets. Such an arrangement will provide a large work surface, with files that are close at hand.

■ If you're working with a carpenter, consider a U-shaped counter with storage underneath. It will provide lots of space conveniently within reach.

■ One compact way is to build work space in a closet. Just close the door when you've finished for the day!

■ If you have a useless cubbyhole in a study, bedroom, living room or even the kitchen, consider building a desk to fit in that area.

You can add shuttered doors to close off the area when it's not in use.

■ When space is at a premium, build a collapsible counter. Make sure you have shelves or a storage unit near by for supplies.

Organising your desk area

■ You must be able to find what you're looking for quickly. 'A place for everything and everything in its place' is an important principle to keep in mind.

■ To avoid having to jump up and down as you work, plan space near by for the following:

- address book or index cards
- birthday book (see Chapter 38)
- computer, monitor, keyboard and mouse mat
- diary (although this should always be with you when you're out on appointments, it should have a 'reserved' space on your desk)
- dictionary
- files
- reference books
- resource files (see Chapter 14)
- telephone and answering machine
- waste-paper basket

■ Materials to have on hand:

- calculator
- chequebook
- clock
- eraser
- paper and envelopes
- household affairs folder (see Chapter 16)
- labels

- letter opener
- notepads
- paper clips
- pens and pencils
- rubber bands
- ruler
- scissors
- stapler
- stamps
- sticky tape

■ Organise the above materials according to use. For example, if you use your letter opener more frequently than your stapler, so place it in a more convenient spot.

■ A bulletin board is a good desk aid, but don't leave notes up until they are yellow with age. The bulletin board should be used for reminders that need to be visible, such as telephone dialling codes you use frequently.

Additional storage

■ Any type of work area can benefit from a storage station on wheels with swing-out drawers, storage bins and trays.

■ Design and have built a shelving unit to go above your desk to keep useful items. The unit should be in the proper proportion to your desk – close to it and low enough to reach without standing up.

■ At a stationery shop, look for desktop organisers to hold the items you won't be putting in drawers. There are units that can hold a few file folders for current projects; others have space for pens and pencils as well as miniature drawers or cups for items such as rubber bands and paper clips. But don't buy so many that you clutter your desk with unnecessary organisers.

Establishing better desk work habits

When it comes to desk organisation, piles of paper are the single biggest problem I see. You don't have time to finish a project, so you leave it until morning. You're expecting an answer from XYZ Company by the end of the week, so you'll leave the file out until then. You didn't finish reading the post, so you'll leave it until Monday. And the only problem is that by the time Monday comes, it's too late because now there is pile after pile after pile, and it seems it would take weeks ever to untangle the mess.

Here are some tips to help you work better.

- The key is not to let paper and piles keep multiplying. Process each paper as it comes in, and get it off your desk.

- Make it a rule to always re-file things. You can establish a special place (such as a desktop file) for current projects, but otherwise put everything away.

- Keep your desk free of clutter. It may tempt your eyes to roam, making time at your desk less effective. Put loose papers in clearly labelled files ('To do', 'To read', and so on) or colour-coded ones (purple = medical, green = legal matters).

- If you're concerned about remembering where you are going to put some notes you'll need for an upcoming project, note the location on your bulletin board or in the tickler file (see Chapter 11) under the day or month the project is due.

- If you have taken files out of dead storage for a specific project, gather them up when the project is completed and take the time to put them back where they belong.

- Establish a Desk Workbook. Buy a medium-sized loose-leaf notebook (you can easily keep the workbook current by simply taking out pages that are no longer relevant), paper and dividers. It is invaluable for recording ideas in the working or development stage. Instead of jotting down notes on scraps of paper and never knowing where to find them, you'll have one place to look when you want to refer back to that million-dollar idea you had the other night. Items found in a Desk Workbook might include a clever paragraph for a sales letter; the punch-line for a speech to be written at the end of the week; a new marketing idea; possible titles for a new project; anecdotes; meeting notes; details of a telephone conversation. Move this information to a file when appropriate. For example, the punch-line for a speech should be moved to a folder labelled 'Speech' once research and writing of the speech is under way. Use the dividers to break the notebook into categories: 'Ideas', 'Business plan', 'Meetings', or whatever you choose).

■ Your Desk Workbook (or the bulletin board) is also a perfect place for an assignment sheet that will keep track of ongoing projects. List the date the assignment was given to you (or when you assigned it to someone else), a description, a progress report, comments and the due date.

■ To keep track of deadlines, use your tickler files (see Chapter 11), computer or diary. Be sure to note a project's deadline on a date earlier than when it is due to make sure you finish it in time.

■ Set aside time daily for doing paperwork. Choose an hour when there are few distractions – if at home, in the early morning before the family gets up; or, if at work, before staff come in. During this time, use an answering machine or your voice-mail system to screen the calls, ask for calls to be held or ask a colleague to answer your phone (you can return the favour at another time).

■ Use your desk clock as an important ally. If you're procrastinating about something, tell yourself you'll work on it for 'just 15 minutes'. And use the clock to help you stop early enough so you will have time to put things away at the end of the day.

■ Clean up your desk every night so there's no chaos when you begin the next morning.

What to do when your desk is a disaster

Many of my clients are frantic because their desks are such a mess. They can't find slips of paper on which they wrote important phone numbers;

they know they received information they sent for, but now it's buried in a pile of paper; they were working on a chapter of a novel, but now the notes for the next chapter are gone.

Here's how I counsel them when I make a 'house call'.

- Address your desk problems in blocks of time. You may be able to straighten out the clutter in a few hours, or you may need a weekend. Sometimes it's better to devote a couple of hours a day to the job until it's done.

- Have on hand a waste-paper basket, a pen, file folders, labels and any other desk organisational aids I have discussed above that suit your needs.

- Clear the space you want to organise (the desk surface, one of the drawers, etc.), then make a big pile of all the paper.

- Evaluate each item, categorise it and put it away (in the desk drawer, in a file, in one of the desk organisers, etc.), throwing out as much as possible (see Chapter 11).

- Even when you are feeling overwhelmed, just keep sorting and categorising. If you devote the necessary time, your desk can be cleared.

- Re-read this chapter's 'Establishing better desk work habits' periodically. The tips offer the key to keeping your desk clear once you're there.

11

Filing Systems

Most people have trouble with filing. I once had a client who was desperate because of an overflow of paper. She finally took to carrying all her important papers in a bag everywhere she went. 'I didn't want to put them down at home because I was afraid I wouldn't be able to find them again,' she said.

So much material bombards us in this information-filled world that it is often overwhelming to sort through it all and store it for future reference. The solution is a personal filing system that will store all relevant information you and your family may need. I can help you create that system – I've done it for the desperate, and it will work for you, too.

So whether you've turned to this chapter because you're drowning in piles of paper or whether you have a fairly organised system that you just don't keep up, there is hope. It will take perseverance and some time, but there is a way to create a filing system for home or office where it will take you no more than five minutes to locate a piece of paper, no matter how long it's been since you last saw it.

Common filing mistakes

There are three common mistakes people make when filing:

- They fall into the 'Now where would I have filed that?' syndrome. By not establishing a logical system, they have trouble remembering how to find what they've filed.

- They establish a workable system – but don't keep up with it. If you have more than 10 or 12 pieces of paper waiting to be filed, you've fallen into the 'I'll do it tomorrow' trap.

- People file 'in perpetuity'. Just because you thought a certain piece of paper might come in handy after university, there may be no good reason still to have it on hand 10 years later.

Establishing a system

The most effective filing system is one that is:

- simple;
- easy to understand;
- easily accessible to anyone.

You don't want a system that is so complicated that you or others will need written instructions to figure it out.

- First, set aside time to re-organise your system. If you have a limited number of items to be filed, it may take half a day. If you have extensive home files, plan to spend three days or so (or an hour a day for two or three weeks).
- Next, invest in a good, sturdy filing cabinet. Whether it is a one- or a four-drawer unit depends on your filing needs. Allow room for growth!
- Finally, plan that your files will ultimately be stored near your work station.

Alphabetical or colour-coded?

There are two simple systems for establishing a filing system. Both are quite workable.

- Alphabetical. The key element here is choosing appropriate titles so that the folder will be where you expect it to be. For example, if you're starting a file for ideas for a new career, should you call the file 'New job', 'Career ideas', or 'New career'? This will obviously make a difference in how the folder gets alphabetised. How to decide? Title it as you most often think of or talk about it. Listen to yourself for a few days and note how you refer to the subject. If you say to a friend, 'I'm thinking of looking for a new job,' then 'New job' would probably be the best title for the file.
- Colour-coding. Decide on a colour system that will work best for you; for example, pick a different colour for each member of your family. These colours should be consistent throughout the home: John's toothbrush, towels, etc. – as well as his file folders

– could be red. Or you can use this system for different subjects: insurance is green, travel information is blue, and so on. Colour-coding speeds filing and acts as insurance against mis-filing. Your memory responds to colour first, so when you want the insurance folder, you automatically think 'green'. Apply this colour scheme to the files themselves by using coloured folders and file labels or tabs so you can easily pick out the proper colour and category.

■ Make a colour key that will explain the system to everyone who wishes to use the file, and have the key within easy access.

Some people do a combination of alphabetical and colour-coding. The coloured folders are filed alphabetically. It makes retrieval within the file drawer easier. In my filing system, any client-related informa-tion is stored in blue folders, and each folder is filed alphabetically by the client's last name.

Step one: getting started

■ Have to hand a pen or marker, file folders, and file labels that match the colour of your file folders.

■ Choose a work area with plenty of space.

■ Gather together all the miscellaneous papers you want to file as well as any existing files you may have.

■ Evaluate the type of information you want to keep to begin developing file categories. Of course, the categories will vary according to your interest or work requirements, but they will probably include some or many that are listed below. (These categories are primarily for the home.) Following each category, I have included some of the items which might be filed there. (As discussed previously, the exact title you choose for each file is the one that will work best for you.)

• Bargains – the best places to shop for certain items, articles about discounted items.

• Car – payment or leasing details, owner's manual, log

book, MOT certificate, tax certificate.

- Cash receipts – receipts for major purchases such as appliances, jewellery, furniture, home maintenance equipment, as well as your 'New purchases' list for the year.
- Consumer information – articles on consumerism and listings of whom to contact for various problems.
- Contracts – agreements between you and people who work for you or for whom you work.
- Correspondence – letters you want to keep for reference (each family member should have a separate file).
- Credit card records – list of credit card account numbers with name, address and phone number to contact in case the card is stolen; statements and direct debit details.
- Employment – past and present CVs, pay slips, contracts, pension records from previous employers.
- Financial planning – budget-related items, financial goals, financial planning articles.
- Gift lists – lists of gifts given in previous years as well as an ongoing list for the current year.
- Guarantees and warranties – certificates, instruction manuals, lists of authorised service centres.
- Hobbies – articles or information about your leisure interests.
- House, owned – receipts for home improvement work, contracts, mortgage details.
- House, rented – copy of the rental agreement, inventory, pictures showing the condition of the property when you moved in.
- Important documents – photocopies of documents such as birth certificates, passports, marriage licence, divorce papers; originals should be kept in a safe-deposit box (see Chapter 21). Photocopies of family wills (originals are sometimes kept by your solicitor). Your National Insurance card and driving licence. Information regarding the

whereabouts of important documents, and names and addresses of personal advisors – all of which are contained on your Financial Master List (see Chapter 18).

- Insurance – copies of all policies; list of policy numbers, names of insured persons and possessions, issuing company, agent, type and amount of coverage. Personal Property Inventory (see Chapter 20) including original purchase price of valuable items, model and serial numbers, and photos showing especially valuable or unusual possessions. (Keep another copy of this inventory in your safe and one in a safe-deposit box.)

- Interior design – names of recommended designers, articles about interior design, photos of other homes you like.

- Investments – records of buying and selling of stocks and shares, and bonds; broker's purchase and sales statements; statements showing broker's commission.

- Medical history records – history of family illnesses (see Chapter 12). Each family member should have a separate colour-coded file.

- Reviews of restaurants and films – articles giving recommendations.

- Trust information – correspondence and copies of documents relating to any trusts held. (Original documents should be stored in a safe-deposit box.)

- Volunteer work – material and correspondence relating to any volunteer organisation with which you work.

Step two: the process

- Overwhelming as it may seem, go through the stack of papers you've collected piece by piece, making a decision about where to file each paper. Try to handle each paper only once.

- As you evaluate each item, your first questions should be, 'Do I really need to save this? If I needed the information, could I get it elsewhere?'

- Next ask, 'How do I plan to use this information?' and not, 'Where should I put this?' For example, the business card of someone you met from Cardiff might be filed in 'Travel', rather than with other business cards, because you hope to visit him there.

- If you're stuck, put that piece of paper aside and review it again when you've finished processing the others. Where it belongs may be clearer later.

- Keep working through your papers until you've completely finished. It may take several hours or days, but it will be worth it. You'll have an organised system that will work well for you.

Step three: develop good filing habits

- Depending on the file, there are different ways of organising within it. For example, the information in a file of correspondence with one company (perhaps concerning a complaint) might best be filed chronologically, with the most recent letter on top. The information in a file of correspondence with many companies would best be filed alphabetically by company. Choose the system that makes sense for each of your files.

- Staple, rather than clip, relevant material together. Paper clips tend to catch on other papers.

- Store each ongoing activity and project in its own file folder, clearly labelled so you don't have to go through the file to see what's in it. Sometimes people make the mistake of assuming they can stack something on their desk since they'll be finished with it 'soon'. You'll be much happier if there's 'a place for everything, and everything in its place'.

- Divide larger projects into several folders to facilitate retrieval. For example, your work organising a conference might be broken down into 'Conference publicity', 'Conference brochure', 'Conference mailing lists'.

- If you've had a difficult time deciding where to file a certain piece of paper, consider cross-referencing between two (or more) files. Put a reference slip in each file where the paper could have been filed, telling the actual location of the item. This is more efficient (and less bulky) than making multiple copies of something which might fit into one of several categories.

- If you must have the complete copy in another file (for example, something you want on file at home and at the office), make a photocopy.

- If you must remove papers from a file for any period of time, leave a note saying where they have gone.

- Keep frequently used files in an accessible spot.

Step four: maintain your filing system

- File regularly. Have a tray or create a 'To file' folder. Establish a set time to file, at least twice a week, and preferably daily. The more often you file, the less time it takes.

- Keep files lean and current by moving out information you haven't worked on in six months or more. Establish 'Inactive' project files (appropriately titled) and store them in an accessible spot, maybe the bottom drawer of a filing cabinet, or a cardboard file box in a cupboard, but make sure you don't mix them in with your active files.

- The easiest way to maintain a file is to sift through it every time you get it out and throw away material you no longer need. This way you can easily maintain your files with little or no effort.

- If there are files you do not use regularly, choose a time once every three months or so to look through them and weed out the items you no longer need. If you find whole files you won't be needing soon, place them in inactive storage.

Establishing 'tickler files'

'Tickler files' for items you want to be reminded of are invaluable to being organised. The files are designed to 'tickle' your memory and keep track of details you don't want to think about or have on your desk until needed.

- You will need 18 file folders. Of these, 12 should be labelled for each month of the year, five should be reserved for each day of the business week (Monday to Friday), and the sixth and final folder should be labelled 'Weekend'. If you're setting up a system for your office, you'll want 12 monthly folders and 31 additional ones, one for each day of the month so that you can slip in notes and materials for meetings or conferences throughout the month.

- The monthly tickler files will remind you of long-term items. You can date-file your optician's business card in order to be reminded to make an appointment to see him in January; or perhaps you've been told to follow up on something in six weeks – all these reminders should be placed in the appropriate monthly tickler file. You may want to keep an index card reminding you of upcoming birthdays on file here (see Chapter 38). I also note down on a card when I should expect an insurance renewal, and I file it in the appropriate month. Other items to be date-filed here might include a pet's yearly vaccination schedule, a note about family medical check-ups in September, a reminder to take winter coats out of storage in October, and so on.

- The daily tickler files will help you organise the papers you need for projects to be done on a certain day. A postcard you receive on Saturday notifying you of a dental appointment you will have to change should be put in Monday's file to remind you to call and make a new appointment. An article you want to send to your mother might be filed under Wednesday – the day you plan to write to her. A note about a question for your insurance agent whom you need to call on Thursday should go in that day's file. A marketing questionnaire you plan to fill in while waiting for your son to take his piano lesson on Tuesday should be filed appropriately. Weekend files might hold such items as films to be developed, photos to be framed, or a note about the kind of seeds you want to look for at the garden centre. As you take care of each item on the appropriate day, discard the reminder. If for some reason you are unable to process something, select another day in which to file it, and take care of it on that day. (Make it a top priority if you've had to delay it once.)

Don't bother to file

- All the business cards you receive. While you'll want to put valuable contacts in your address book, many people who give you their card you'll never see again. Bind such cards together with a rubber band and store the bundle in your Resource File (see Chapter 14). If you eventually do want to contact someone, you can retrieve the appropriate card and create a 'contact' card for them. Otherwise, you can look through the collection periodically and throw away the ones you don't expect to need any longer.
- Papers or cuttings you don't really need. If in doubt, throw it out. It probably won't come in handy.
- Catalogues, mailshots or junk mail that (being realistic) you know you won't refer to.
- Duplicates of anything.
- Information that is obsolete, such as property prices of three years ago or old restaurant reviews
- Chain letters.
- Fliers people insist you take.
- Old notes.

12

Health Records

Everyone should keep a complete record of their own medical history, and parents, of course, must assume responsibility for their children's health records. The history of any diseases or illnesses you've had is important to any medical professional who serves you. In addition, you need to keep records about your reaction to various medicines. If a new doctor needs to prescribe an antibiotic for you, he or she will need to know which ones (if any) have caused negative reactions.

Establishing a system

- For filing purposes, each family member should have his or her own colour (see Chapter 11).
- Buy index cards in the appropriate colours or use white cards with appropriately coloured file labels to denote each family member's colour. You could also store the information on your computer, but it might be a good idea to create and file a print-out too.
- On each person's card, record the following information about significant illnesses or doctor's visits:

MEDICAL RECORD	JOHN JONES		
Date/Doctor	Reason for visit	Medication (and instruction) or immunisation	Reaction

- For adult family members, keep an accurate record of illnesses or health problems severe enough to merit a visit to the doctor. For your own information, note frequent colds or headaches and your reactions to various types of over-the-counter drugs. If you need to see a doctor for persistent headaches, you'll have accurate information, or if you want to know which cold remedy doesn't make you sleepy, you can check your notes.

- For children, note immunisations and major illnesses such as chickenpox so that later in life your children will have a medical history to which they can refer. While you may not want to keep track of each time your child goes for a check-up, it will be helpful, for example, to note the date of an ear infection and what medication was used. Then, if the illness recurs, you'll know what medicine your child was given and how effective it was. If you have more than one child, a written record of this information is vital! There's no guarantee that you'll remember who reacted badly to a certain antibiotic or who had chickenpox five summers ago.

- Store these cards or the computer print-out in your Health Records File in your filing cabinet.

13

Post, E-Mail, and Faxes

The post

I've nicknamed the daily arrival of the post 'information blues time'. It can feel as though you are drowning in paper. What's more, there's no stopping it. Through rain, sleet, snow and hail the postman is going to continue to contribute to your growing pile of unread post. When it comes to post management, remember the following.

Rule number one: you must deal with the post daily. As few as 15 minutes each day is painless compared with what you may face if you let it pile up.

Rule number two: don't shuffle the post. Make a decision about each item as you handle it and then follow through.

In addition, the following are specific ways you can successfully fight the daily deluge.

To start

- Choose a specific time and place to process your post, and have a large waste-paper basket handy.
- At home, sort the post according to family member. Your stacks will be more readily manageable if you go through the magazines and catalogues first and then add letters to the top of each pile.
- Establish a set spot for leaving each person's post so he or she will know where to look for it each day.
- If a family member is away, store his or her post in a big brown envelope so there will be no chance of misplacing anything.

- Next, sort your own post using the following categories:

    - to throw away;
    - to ask about;
    - to file;
    - to call;
    - to do;
    - to read.

Here are strategies for coping with items in each category.

To throw away

- Instead of asking yourself, 'Could I possibly use this one day?' ask, 'What's the worst thing that could happen if I throw this out?' If the answer is 'nothing', then throw it away.

- Make a game out of seeing how much you can throw away before you reach a certain spot. If you live in a block of flats and pick up post in the entrance hall, try to pull out as much 'junk' as you can before you reach the door of your flat. If you live in a house, try to pull out as much as possible before reaching a designated spot, such as the kitchen waste-paper basket.

- At the office, go through the pile quickly, throwing out everything that you know isn't even worth opening.

- Tear up the letters you throw out so that you won't be tempted to retrieve them. I haven't had a client yet who hasn't gone back into the trash to rescue something he or she couldn't live without. Should you ever throw away something you later need (a rare occurrence in my experience), you'll probably be able to get another copy.

- If unwanted junk mail is the source of your post overload problem, write to any companies with whom you correspond (mail-order companies, credit card companies, magazines) and insist that they do not give your name to others. Create a standard letter to save time. When you answer ads, or enter competitions, make sure you tick the special box which protects your right not to have your details passed on to other companies. You can also write to a company called MPS, at Freepost 22, London W1E 7BZ and ask to be removed from mailing lists. Provide variations of your name: John J. Jones, Jack Jones, J. J. Jones, etc. Your name will be put on a list which is circulated among direct-mail companies, who will remove your name from their database. If you are a regular mail-order customer, this may only reduce your post slightly as your name will remain active on lists belonging to companies with whom you choose to do business. You can also put an end to annoying phone calls by writing to MPS, or calling the Direct Mail Association on 0171 3212525.

To ask about

- Place items that require the comments of another person with the rest of that person's post. At home, you may want to check with your partner regarding a dinner invitation; at the office, you may need to pass a letter on to your boss or a colleague.

- Attach a Post-it note, and write down your question – 'Did you make the 26 March purchase? If not, there's a mistake in the statement'; or 'This business luncheon looks interesting. Do you plan to go?' – so that you won't have to re-read it later.

- Staple all relevant information from the same envelope together (travel brochure, agent's business card, price list, etc.) so nothing will get lost.

To file

- Papers that do not require immediate action (insurance policies, tax forms you receive in advance, some legal documents) can be filed.

- Bills should be filed in your Household Affairs Folder under 'Unpaid bills' (see Chapter 16) so they can be paid all at once or just prior to their due date.

- Establish tickler files (see Chapter 11) for those items that can't (or needn't) be resolved immediately. If you're thinking of registering for a class that starts in a month, put the course information in the folder for the appropriate month so that you can consider it as the registration date gets closer. If you've received a flier about a free event that you'd like to attend on Wednesday night, put the notice in Wednesday's folder.

To call

- Can a matter be handled more quickly by phone than by letter?
- If the place you need to contact is closed for the day, put the item on your list of things to do for the next day.
- Remember to group the calls you need to make. It wastes time to scatter them throughout the day.

To do

- The items on your list of things to do are the ones that require action, and several steps may be involved. Start with the most important items first. For example, a returned cheque or an invitation requiring a written RSVP should be acted upon as soon as possible, while renewing a magazine subscription or answering your aunt's monthly letter can wait.

To read

- Be selective. Read only what is important or what interests you.
- Thumb through incoming publications and tear out information of special interest. Throw away the journal or magazine, and keep the articles in a file marked 'On-the-go reading'. Every day, select several articles to carry with you and, whenever you find yourself waiting, pull them out. When you've finished, throw away the item or mark where it should be filed.

Below are some other typical items that arrive in the post and advice on how to handle each one.

- A reminder of a six-month dental check-up. Make sure the appointment is marked in your diary. Confirm the surgery address and phone number, and note them down in your diary next to the appointment. Throw away the reminder.

- A calendar of events for the upcoming concert season. If you're not sure you want to attend, note in your diary (in pencil) any of the dates that interest you. Otherwise, you may book something else for those times. Then put the schedule in your tickler file where you can review it again at a later date. If you need to order tickets by the end of the week, file the schedule in your Friday tickler file. Otherwise, file the schedule in an appropriate monthly tickler file. Just make sure you file it where you'll see it before it's too late. If you need to book by 1 October, for example, file the schedule in the September folder.

- Business correspondence that requires a reply. As you read the letter, circle specific questions as a reminder to answer them. Then jot down key points on the letter itself for you or your secretary to draft a response. Put it on your 'To do' list for the next day.

If you have lots of standard business correspondence, you may find that making a correspondence book will save time. Take paragraphs from the best of your recent correspondence, organise them by subject, and number them. Then you need note only the paragraph numbers you want and your secretary can use his or her copy of the book to write the letters. If your secretary has all the paragraphs on computer, he or she ought to be able to 'build' a letter in just a few moments. It's a fast way of producing accurate, well-written replies!

- Personal correspondence.
  - Phone a reply.
  - Carry notepaper or postcards with you, and write a note when you have a spare moment, while waiting for an appointment, for example.
  - Write one letter and make copies. On the computer you can add some personalisation to a basic letter. Some people do a family update letter during the holiday season. One

woman who was inundated with kind words from many people during a long illness found this was the only way to keep up with her correspondence.

- Change of address note from someone you know. Enter the information in your address book right away and throw away the card.

- Notes informing you of an upcoming meeting you need to attend. Write down the date in your calendar and throw away the letter. Keep the agenda, if there is one, in the appropriate tickler file.

- A piece of post that gives you a good idea for a new project. If you're inspired, start on it now. Otherwise, file it in your tickler file.

- Catalogue from a company you like. Thumb through it and mark the pages with items of interest. Contact the company by post or phone. If you prefer to give your potential purchase a little more thought, put the catalogue in your tickler file under the day or month when you might be in a better position to decide, for example, after paying your bills.

- New catalogue from an unknown company. Scan the first few pages. If the information doesn't catch your interest immediately, throw it away – or even better recycle it!

- Business magazine. Use the 'rip and read' method. Scan the contents (or the magazine) for articles of interest. Tear them out and file them in your 'On-the-go reading' file (see page 67).

- Other magazines (fashion, sports, architectural design). Save these for when you have some spare time. Put them with your leisure reading.

E-mail

In today's world, more and more people are using electronic mail. Many offices depend on it, and if you've got a home computer and subscribe to an online service (see Chapter 9), then you're learning the benefits of using electronic mail for communicating with friends and family.

E-mail is an easy and fast way to correspond, but despite its time-saving efficiency, you've got to guard against it becoming an activity that eats up your time. Because it's so easy, many people are using it to chat, and answering these types of e-mail messages from people you barely know can waste a lot of time. In addition, follow these tips to use e-mail effectively:

- Set aside a specific time each day to answer your e-mail (just as you should your regular post). Scan the incoming messages by order of importance, using the subject line or the sender to make a judgement. If you're running low on time and have not answered all your messages, skim through the remaining list, and do these three things:
  - answer the more important immediately;
  - save the significant for the next day;
  - delete everything else.

- Keep your own messages clear and to the point. Be specific about what you need to know so that the message you get in return will also be concise.

- If you've been away for a few days and are staring at 200 to 250 messages, scan the list and answer in order of priority. You can work on it over a period of a couple of days, or you may decide that some messages just aren't worth answering.

Junk mail exists in electronic form, too. Here's how to stay off the lists.

- Be cautious about giving out your name and e-mail address.
- Check out special services through online services and the Internet to specify that you don't want to be on general mailing lists.
- If you receive unwanted e-mail, notify the senders. They are supposed to remove you from their lists.
- If you're on a circulation list at work and it's not really necessary that you receive all the mailings, ask the sender to remove your name.

■ E-mail addresses should be kept in your online address book so that you can click and send easily, but also note e-mail addresses in your personal address book so that you can stay in touch even when you're not on your own computer.

Faxes at home and at the office

The fax machine is another wonderful invention of the past few years. Text and images travel quickly across telephone wires and are exactly reproduced, either on paper or on a computer screen, at the other end of the wire.

You'll be well used to having and using a fax machine at your office. If you're considering having one at home, the following are a few points to keep in mind.

■ What type of paper does it use? The less expensive machines use thermal paper which comes on rolls and tends to curl. This may be fine for a family who is reading and throwing away personal communications. If you plan to use a fax machine for business purposes, you're better off with a more expensive model that uses plain paper. This will provide you with a better quality of fax to save and refer to over time.

■ Ask about other features. All machines can be used for low-volume copying; some have speed-dialling; many have a memory so that an incoming fax can be stored if you are low on toner or out of paper; many also have a 'broadcast' feature that permits you to send one fax to several different numbers. New machines being created for the home market are also designed to serve as answering machines.

Here are some additional tips for better fax management:

■ If you've also got a modem (see Chapter 9), consider getting a dedicated phone line for the fax and modem. Unless you live alone, trying to manage a telephone, a modem and a fax machine on the same line may lead to a communications block.

■ Fax during off-peak hours. It's cheaper.

- If you're faxing to another time zone, consider the hour there. The receiver who keeps the fax machine in or close to the bedroom may not be thrilled to get your fax at three o'clock in the morning.
- Just because a fax arrives instantly doesn't mean it needs to be answered instantly.
- If junk faxes start arriving, fax back to the sender to remove you from the list. The sender's number usually appears on the fax that comes through to you.

14

Resource File

Have you ever asked yourself, 'I'd really like to get back in touch with that man I met at last year's conference to talk to him about a career change, but I have no idea how to contact him . . .'

A resource file can solve a problem such as this, and others, by providing you with a total system for keeping track of people whom you might like to contact again. Unlike names in a personal telephone directory, these people aren't necessarily individuals you contact regularly, just people you might need one day.

Some people like to integrate this information into their index card system, making notes regarding the services on the back of the cards. Or see Chapter 9 if you'd prefer to put this information on your computer.

Otherwise, here's an efficient way to keep tabs on people and service providers you may want to contact again.

Establishing a resource file

You'll need:

- Index cards in different colours (for example, green for personal contacts, red for home resources, blue for medical, and so on).
- Index card dividers.
- Container for holding index cards.

I like using a card system because each index card provides plenty of room for writing complete information about the person or the service. The system is also easy to update, because you simply add another card if you find someone new, or throw away a card if someone moves or a service goes out of business. In addition, there's always room on the card for adding new details.

- As noted in Chapter 9, an address book on computer offers many of the same advantages of this system. If you're looking for the printer whose name you can't remember, you can key 'printer', and your computer will do the searching for you.

Contact resource cards

- Part of your resource file should consist of cards you make with the names of your personal contacts – people whom you've met at parties or conferences or to whom you've been referred by friends. Whenever you need advice, help or special treatment, you can check the cards to see who might be of help. Update your cards with additional information you get about the person. Add new cards when you make new contacts.

- A typical contact resource card might look like this:

```
Mary Jones              Met at ASPW Conference      11/96
629 North Avenue
Kingsbourne
Hertfordshire

01234 987654

Special knowledge of personnel job market; worked at XYZ
Company for 12 years

Consultancy fee:  £80/hour

Husband:  Mark
Children:  Sam and Alex

20/12/96 Phone conversation: discussed training I would need to
work in personnel field
```

- List why this person is of interest to you; include special knowledge and skills.

- Make sure you write down how you met the person or who referred you to him or her. Also note the date of the first meeting or referral.
- List fees or hourly rates.
- Record the name of husband, wife, children and any other significant family members in order to facilitate personal conversations.
- If the person seems like someone you will get to know better, you may want to find out the date of his or her birthday and make a note of it here.
- List dates and notes about conversations and meetings.
- As you prepare to put your cards into the index card container, you will need two of your card dividers. Label one 'Contacts' and the other 'Home services' (see below). Some people file their cards alphabetically by name within each of these two groupings. Others find that they forget names, so filing by category makes the information more readily accessible. For example, suppose you have some work to be done that soon will require the services of a photographer. You meet one you like but know that you'll never be able to remember his name two months from now. Label an index card divider 'Photographers' and use it to file the card on him and on any other photographers you hear about or meet. If you decide to file by subject rather than by name, be consistent. (An index card divider labelled 'Contacts General' can be a catch-all for those for whom it isn't worth creating a category.)

Home service resource cards

- On each card, list the company (or individual), the business address, telephone, fax and e-mail numbers, exactly what you used their services for (if you have), the date, and how much you paid for the service.
- A sample card might look like this:

REPAIRS—CHINA AND GLASS

AAA Company   Recommended by: Mother 12/96
5 Great Oak Street
London W9

0171 123 9876

Repairs glass and china; specialises in antique porcelain and ceramics; work takes minimum of two weeks

Repaired chipped goblet, January 97, £17.50

- If a resource has come through a recommendation, note who recommended it to you, and the date.
- As you note details, be very specific. For example, one cobbler may be great at replacing heels; or one cleaner may be good at knitwear, while another does the best job on dinner suits.
- Additional resources can be gained by reading articles featured in many magazines. You can note information about those that might be of use and add them to your file.
- Use card dividers to create appropriate categories for your needs, such as cleaners and painters.

Once you've set up a 'Home services' resource file, you will soon find it invaluable. Being able rapidly to locate all the home services you need will save you hours of telephoning and searching for the right person to fix your iron or the right shop to go to for a certain type of cleaning liquid.

Financial Records

15

Banking

From an organisational standpoint, there are two major difficulties when it comes to banking. The first concerns the chaos that can ensue if your chequebook and records are not kept up to date. An accurate, well-maintained chequebook can reduce your risk of a bank error going unnoticed, and it can save you a lot of aggravation at tax time.

The second type of difficulty involves the time that can be wasted while trying to get your personal banking done. How often have you fumed because the queue at the bank was so long? I have some tips to help you with that, too.

Today your life can be greatly simplified by taking advantage of the various automatic services your bank offers, and you should also know about electronic banking. It's the way of the future.

Establishing a system

- When it comes to efficient record-keeping, one of the most important decisions to make is your choice of chequebook. I recommend using a larger desk-style chequebook simply because it provides more room for explaining each cheque or deposit.

- Clients frequently protest, 'But what about the cheques I need to write when I'm away from home?' The solution is simple. When you order your desk-style chequebook, also order a small number of cheques in the small format, and use that when you are on the go. Because you have an entire chequebook with you, you are automatically reminded to record the cheque. Then make it a habit to note the date, cheque number, payee, the reason for the expenditure, and the amount in your main (desk-style) chequebook when you do your daily paperwork that evening. I find that people who carry a single cheque with them often forget to record it when they get home. One man I know takes a cheque with him in the morning, uses it, and then forgets to write down the amount for which he wrote it. His wife says he regularly wastes time bemoaning the fact that he can't remember how much the cheque was for. The second chequebook will solve that.

■ Deposits should also be carefully noted, and on each deposit slip, note the source of the income, so that you can include it on your tax return.

■ Balance your main chequebook after each entry so that you have an accurate view of your current bank balance. (You need not balance your auxiliary chequebook since it reflects only a portion of the cheques you write.)

■ Keep all your deposit slips and cheque stubs in a folder until you need them to balance your chequebook. When your statement arrives, compare your slips against the bank's record, and once each withdrawal and deposit is verified, you can put the slips with the appropriate statements.

■ When your statement comes, balance your account right away. The longer you wait, the more complex it will become because you will have to account for additional cheques and deposits.

■ Tick cheques and deposits that are verified and mark those that have not yet appeared on the bank statement.

■ At the end of the year, the cheque stubs, deposit slips and statements should be stored with your Household Affairs Folder (see page 83) where they will be easily accessible yet out of the way.

■ It is generally recommended that you keep banking records for at least six years; business-related records may need to be kept longer.

Personal banking

If you are looking around for a new bank, you'll need to consider what services are offered and what rates are charged, and how efficiently your transactions will be handled. Whether or not the bank will make life easier for you is almost as important as the services they offer and how much it will cost you.

- Is the bank part of a large network of banks so that you'll have access to cashpoint machines almost everywhere you go?

- Are there always long queues at your branch of the bank? How quickly can you have a meeting with someone if you have a problem?

- If you need to do banking in person, visit the bank during periods of least activity, which vary according to the branch and its location. Generally, it's best to avoid lunch hours and paydays, and Monday mornings.

- Most companies can arrange to have your salary paid directly into your account. This way, you get the money instantly, and you needn't go to the bank to deposit it.

- Have your deposit and withdrawal slips already made out – and handy – before you go to the bank. You will save time and perhaps be more accurate since you've made them out in the privacy and quiet of your home or office.

- If your bank is one of those who are charging for each transaction or withdrawal from the cashpoint machine, try to plan ahead to limit the number of times you need to use these services. This will also save time.

Taking advantage of bank services

- Your bank can take care of regular payments (such as mortgage or insurance payments) for you via direct debit. This saves you considerable worry and time.

- Are you interested in banking by phone? More and more banks are using systems by which you can check your balance, verify deposits, confirm cheque payouts, stop payment on a cheque, get a summary of transactions, and pay bills, all by making a simple phone call. Ask about these at your bank or pick up a brochure.

Online banking

If you've got a home computer with a modem, you may be able to do a great deal of banking from the comfort of your own home. (Your computer can do almost everything that a cashpoint machine does, except give out cash.) The at-home banking services make it easy to download bank transactions, transfer funds, reconcile chequebooks, and pay bills online. Some are offering the availability of credit card account review, and some have facilities for you to buy and sell shares as well. Costs are reasonably low, and banks foresee a day when cyberspace banking will replace the need for a 'bank on every corner'.

This new style of banking is particularly popular with people who are already computer-literate, and with frequent travellers, who appreciate the convenience of being able to monitor their finances while they are away.

- If you opt for online banking, there are currently two variations to the services:
  - Some services are offered through banks, and to operate them you generally need to obtain the bank's proprietary software (sometimes made available free of charge to encourage you to use the service). This permits you to see account information, make transfers between accounts and pay bills.
  - Online banking is also available through some types of personal finance software. By entering your chequebook expenses and miscellaneous cash expenditures, this software will track your cash flow, help plan a personalised budget for your family, and provide you with helpful data for tax purposes. However, to use it for online banking, your bank must offer an interface with the software you've selected.

- Before purchasing any software, talk to someone at your bank about your bank's electronic capabilities.

- Keep in mind that there is currently a delay of 12 to 24 hours between you performing any banking transaction (paying a bill, transferring funds, etc.) and it actually being posted to your account, so don't expect to do anything at the last minute.

16

Paying Bills

Perhaps you can identify with a friend of mine who was saying how much he enjoys a good meal or a fun night out, but finds it 'so depressing when it comes to paying the bills . . .'

As you know, the only thing worse than paying a bill is discovering that you didn't pay it and are now being fined or charged interest. Time and again, I visit clients who have left their bills in piles of unopened post; others have thrown out store card statements thinking they were junk mail. One woman simply stuffed her bills under a cushion. Needless to say, these bill-paying 'methods' can be costly.

This chapter provides you with a simple and effective system for paying your bills. You'll even learn how to do it electronically. The organisational tips provided or the possibility of doing it online should make bill-paying less painful.

Setting up a household affairs folder

- Visit a stationery shop and buy a folder to store your yet-to-be-billed shopping receipts, your unpaid bills, and your copies of the bills you have paid.
- Mark the outside of the folder with the current year.
- Divide the folder into sections with categories such as bank records, car, income taxes, insurance records, medical/dental, receipts, rent and mortgage records, utilities, unpaid bills, and so on, using stick-on file folder labels.

Sorting bills, receipts, and solicitations

- Keep receipts for items you have charged to a card in a small envelope within the Receipts section. The envelope keeps everything together for eventual cross-checking with the bill and allows you to thumb quickly through the envelope to find out just how much you have paid for by credit card at any given time.

■ When a bill arrives in the post, open it. Pull out your receipts and make sure that all charges are correct. If not, you have time to straighten it out before the bill is due. If action is necessary, phone or write to the company. If all is in order, cheque the due date and put the bill back in its original envelope. Mark the due date on the outside of the envelope. File it in chronological order in the Unpaid Bills section of your household affairs folder.

■ If you receive a request for a donation from a charity that interests you, file it in the Unpaid Bills section as well. (After covering other costs, you will be better able to evaluate how much you want to give and to whom.)

Establishing a system

■ Assign one member of the family to be in charge of bill-paying. My husband and I take six-month stints at the job, but most families find it works better if just one person pays the bills all the time.

■ Choose a set time twice a month for bill-paying and allow approximately 30 minutes for it. You may be wondering why you can't do it just once a month. There are three reasons. First, bills arrive throughout the month, and if you've only established one bill-paying period, you may find that you'll end up always making late payments. Second, by paying once every two weeks, you can pay closer to the date that the money is actually due. That gives you the use of your money for a longer period of time rather than letting the company earn interest on it. And finally, not many chequebooks can withstand one major bill-paying assault. By paying twice a month you have allowed a little cash to flow in before it needs to flow out again.

■ Establish a set place (your desk or the kitchen table, for example) for paying your bills.

- Have on hand a pen, your chequebook, a few extra envelopes, return address labels, stamps, a wastebasket, and your household affairs folder.

The process

- Remove all the bills and requests from the Unpaid Bills section of the folder. Pull out the ones that you need to post soon.

- If you did not do so when the bills arrived, you will need to cross-cheque the bill with your receipts. Take out the envelope of receipts from the Receipts section of the folder. For all bills, compare your shopping receipts with the actual charges. Make sure that all amounts charged are correct and that there are no extra charges about which you have questions.

- As you write the cheque, make sure you date it, correctly identify the payee, fill in the correct amount, and sign it with your legal signature. Some cheques should carry additional identifying information. A cheque to a department store should have your account number; a payment to the phone company should have your phone number; a credit card payment should have your credit card number.

- When it comes to payments such as insurance, note your policy number, the type of insurance (car, household or health) and the time period that the payment covers on both the cheque and in your chequebook. Sometimes the computer continues to produce bills even when you've paid them. This record will tell you whether you're up to date on your payments for different policies.

- Once the bill is paid, send off the cheque and the company's portion of the invoice in the envelope provided (or use one of your own, if necessary).

- Mark your portion 'paid' and put the date of payment and the cheque number on it. If you aren't paying the entire amount, note the amount that you did pay. Then transfer your part of the invoice or statement to the appropriate category in the household affairs folder.

- For insurance purposes (see Chapter 20), it is helpful to create a list of major purchases such as jewellery, camera equipment, electronic equipment and other household items of value; bill-paying time is a good opportunity to look after these records. You may want to check with your insurance broker what constitutes a 'major' purchase. On a sheet of paper or a document on your computer, write 'New Purchases' and the year. As you make purchases throughout the year, note those that are over a certain amount (the figure recommended by your insurance broker), and after you've paid the bill, take the receipt for each item and store it in an envelope along with your inventory list. These records should be placed in your Cash Receipts file in your filing cabinet for the rest of the current year; at the end of the year they should be moved to your safe. The records should be retained for the life of the items.

- Information and receipts relating to the purchase of property and payments for any home improvements should be retained until you sell the property. Move these receipts into a permanent file rather than leaving them in your household affairs folder. After paying house-related bills, remove these records and receipts and file them in your Housing file in your filing cabinet (see Chapter 11).

- Now take a look at any requests you may have received from charity. Do you have £50 to send to XYZ Charity? If so, write out the cheque and send it to them.

- Keep a running total of your bank balance. (If you've computerised your personal finances, this is taken care of for you.) Too many people enter the amount of the cheque but neglect to do the calculations to balance the total. This makes it all too easy to go overdrawn by accident.

- Seal and stamp your envelopes. If they need to be posted the next day, put them near the front door.

Electronic bill-paying

If you're used to paying bills just before the due date, you may have wished there were a way you could 'zap' the money straight to the company. Well, today that wish can almost come true, give or take a day or so, with electronic banking.

Electronic bill-paying dispenses with stamps, envelopes and cheques by giving you the ability to pay your bills through your computer and modem if you have special software. The software that is dispensed by your bank, or a type that interfaces with the software your bank's computer uses, provides you with cheque-writing capabilities. Once the electronic cheque is sent via modem, your current account is debited and the money is deposited to the payee through an electronic transfer. (If computerised bill-paying is not available through your bank, there are also online bill-payment services that provide the access you need to pay bills electronically.)

Programs have been designed so that writing a cheque on your computer is very similar to writing out a paper cheque. The difference is in the sending; one cheque leaves your household electronically, while the other must be taken to the post box.

- Before deciding to use the service offered by your bank, check on its track record and reliability. Though most companies promise to resolve any problems and cover any late fees, you don't really want to have to deal with a bank that isn't processing your payments on time.

- Contact your bank and ask for an application. You'll need to choose a personal identification number and may have to send in a voided printed cheque for verification. In return, you'll get an account number and a local modem access number to use for transmitting payments.

- When you're ready to make a payment, you'll feel at home because software designers have created the system so that you enter information much as if you were writing a regular cheque.

- The first time you make a payment will be more time-consuming than later because you'll need to provide the address and account number for each payee. Once the payee is part of your permanent record, you'll need to enter only the payee's name and the amount you intend to pay.

■ This system provides you with more control over your money than the traditional method of bill-paying because you specify the day on which you want the money transferred. You can keep the money in your account for as long as is reasonable and then release it. Experience shows that you need to allow from two to six business days for the transaction to occur, so don't wait until the day the bill is due to pay it.

■ Keep watching for new developments in this area. The possibilities are quite intriguing, and ultimately, the systems are going to be easier and easier to use. Eventually you'll find it hard to believe that you ever wrote out cheques by hand.

What to do at the end of the year

Your household affairs folder will serve as a perfect record of your expenditures during any given calendar year and should be saved. Here's what to do:

■ In early December, buy a new household affairs folder.

■ At the end of December, take out any materials from the old folder that should be transferred to the new one (unpaid bills, loan information, etc.).

■ Close up the old folder and put it in an oversized envelope or expandable folder along with your cheque stubs for the year, and any other relevant information. Label the folder with the appropriate year, and keep it somewhere accessible for the time being, as you will need some of the documentation for your tax return. Once this has come and gone, you can move the folder to dead storage in your attic or cellar.

■ While some items need to be kept for only three years, tax-related receipts and information need to be kept for six, so it's a good idea to wait the full six years before cleaning out your household affairs folder.

17

Budgeting

The purpose of this chapter is to help you establish a simple record-keeping system that will give you a better understanding of the whereabouts of your money.

If you're using a computer, most personal-finance software provides everything you need to categorise your cash flow for better budgeting. However, the financial goal-setting and entry of the information are still up to you.

Setting goals

- Set a long-term goal – 'I want to buy a house in a couple of years . . .'

- Establish short-term goals, with rewards. Sometimes people make the mistake of setting only a long-term goal. The problem with this is that it's easy to get discouraged – it can take months or a year or more before you begin to reap any rewards from it. Instead, establish short-term goals with rewards: if you maintain your budget for two consecutive months, treat yourselves to a special dinner at a restaurant (one that is within your budget); 'If I save £500, I'll buy myself a new sweater for £30.' Such goals make budgeting easier in the short run.

Establishing a system

- Income. Surprisingly, many people don't know exactly what their actual income is. The following chart can help you document your monthly income (both income and expenses are worked out on a monthly basis). Note take-home pay for both partners, part-time income ('moonlighting'), and all other money your family receives regularly. For amounts that come in annually, such as a company bonus, divide the amount received by 12 to arrive at a monthly figure.

- Expenses. Next, you need to determine your expenses. For our purposes, fixed expenses are costs you must pay each month. Variable expenses include the costs of items such as clothing, holidays and entertainment; they are often necessary but you may not incur them every month. Note that some expenses might be fixed for one family and variable for another; where both parents work outside the home, child care is an unavoidable expense. If, however, only one parent works and child care expenses consist of paying for babysitting a few times a month, that cost might be considered variable. Be sure to average in quarterly or annual payments such as insurance premiums, taxes or yearly visits to the doctor. For example, if one of your insurance premiums is £200 per year, you need to set aside £16.67 (£200 divided by 12) in order to cover that expense.

- Personal allowance. Note that this is listed as a fixed rather than variable expense. Each family member should be allotted a reasonable amount of discretionary money if family budgeting is to be successful. If you begin to feel deprived, you might be tempted to dip into money you're earmarking for other things. For children, having a personal allowance introduces them to some of the challenges of managing money.

- Savings. This is also listed as a fixed expense. For everyone, saving something (even as little as £30 per month) should be a top priority. Almost everyone encounters a 'rainy day' at some point, so don't put yourself in the position of saying, 'I wish I'd saved!' When you pay your rent or mortgage, you should get in the habit of automatically writing a cheque to your savings account. By treating savings as a fixed expense, you can guarantee that you'll have money for something special or for when you need it.

- Now work through the budget on page 94, adding items as necessary.

Identifying trouble spots

- Now that you have one total for your spendable income and another for expenses, subtract your expenses from your income to see how you come out. If you're fortunate, your income will exceed your expenses and you will have a 'surplus', which you can divert to savings. However, for many people, expenses exceed income, which means they must economise. For example, your food budget might include a take-away one night a week. Consider getting a take-away just once a month until you get expenses more in line with your income. Review each item under expenses and see where else you can save. But be realistic! Don't stop all magazine subscriptions if you have one or two publications you really enjoy; just cut the costs of the ones you don't read so eagerly any more. We cut down on two subscriptions when our twins were born because we knew we were unlikely to have the time to read much with two babies.

- If you are significantly over-extended, you may need a financial counsellor to help you consolidate your debt. In the process, you should also think long and hard about how to bring your lifestyle more in line with your income.

- Watch your cash. For many people, weekly cash expenditures are a real problem, primarily because they just don't know where the money has gone . . . Maybe you've allotted yourself £50 personal spending money for the week, but somehow by Friday or Saturday, you're dipping into next week's money because you just don't have anything left. Try slipping an index card into your purse or wallet. Every time you spend cash on an item, note down how much you spend and on what. At the end of the week, most people discover they have a weakness for something that they have totally forgotten about: perhaps it's paperbacks or CDs, or lunch in a restaurant a couple of times a week. Whatever it is, once you're aware that your habit is proving costly, you'll be able to cut back on those expenses if you want to.

JANUARY 1997			
Expenses	Date	Cheque no. (if applicable)	Amount
Fixed			
Child care			
Council tax			
Debts (existing)			
or loans			
Education			
Food			
Housing			
(rent/mortgage)			
Income tax			
Insurance			
Car			
Health			
Household			
Life			
Medical/Dental			
Personal allowance			
Savings			
Transport			
Utilities			
Electricity			
Gas			
Telephone			
Water			
Variable			
Charitable donations			
Clothing			
Domestic help			
Entertainment/leisure			
Gifts			
Holiday expenses			
Home maintenance			
and furniture			
Medication			
Savings for holidays			
Other			

Charting monthly expenses

With this system there's no more 'sneaky spending'. I've visited many clients who buy major items, and try to keep the purchase a secret from their partner, using what I call the 'I'm-going-to-fool-*you* way'. They put part of the cost on a credit card, pay for part of it in cash, and write out a cheque for the rest. Other clients sometimes buy things in the 'I'm-going-to-fool-*me* way', by putting a big purchase on a payment plan so that it doesn't seem so costly month to month. Of course, in both cases, the money is spent, and with the second method, it's spent *and* you usually have to pay interest in addition. This system of using the chart to track expenses will keep the whole family honest and help you come to terms with exactly where your money goes each month.

Keeping it up

With some practice, you'll find that budgeting can become a matter of habit, and you'll probably find that paperwork will be unnecessary. Until then, keep a monthly record (like the one above) of exactly what you're spending in each category. Later, a quick glance through your chequebook will show you where the money for that month has gone. And by the way, even cash withdrawals should note: '£30 groceries'; '£25 spending money.'

- Be sure to budget for the unexpected. It's better to have extra money at the end of the year rather than be caught short when extra bills come in.

- Review your budget every six months to make sure it is still serving your needs.

- Keep your goals and your budget realistic, and you'll find that budgeting is well worth the effort.

MONTHLY BUDGET

Income		Expenses	
		Fixed	
Husband's take-home pay	————	Savings	————
Wife's take-home pay	————	Housing (rent or mortgage payments)	————
Moonlighting	————	Taxes, income (if not withheld)	————
Company bonus (as it would average into monthly income)	————	Taxes, property (money set aside for annual payments)	————
		Insurance	
		Auto	————
		Disability	————
Dividends	————	Health	————
Interest	————	Life	————
		Utilities	
Other (profit-sharing, pension, royalties, trust, etc.)	————	Gas and electricity	————
		Water	————
		Telephone	————
Total:	————	Food	————
		Transportation	————
		Child care	————
		Medical/Dental	————
		Education	————
		Debts or loans (car payments, etc.)	————
		Personal allowance	————
		Variable	
		Drug items	————
		Clothing	————
		Home maintenance and furniture	————
		Entertainment/recreation	————
		Domestic help	————
		Charitable donations	————
		Vacation savings	————
		Holiday expenses (gifts)	————
		Other	————
		Total:	————

18

Financial Master List

There are two occasions when having a master list of your financial information is especially helpful. The first occurs when items are lost or missing – credit cards stolen, personal papers or insurance policies destroyed in a fire. The second happens in the event of death or incapacity. At such a stressful time, you should not have to worry about locating either those items that may be needed immediately, or those that will be needed shortly, such as financial papers and insurance policies.

Gathering important numbers

If documents are lost, it is much easier to replace them if you have a list of identifying numbers. This information is also helpful to an executor settling an estate. Such numbers should include the following.

- Bank account numbers, details of your local branch.
- Credit card numbers, and the telephone number to call if a card is lost or stolen.
- Driving licence number.
- Insurance policy numbers, details of insurance companies and of the broker.
- Premium bond numbers.
- National Insurance numbers for each family member.
- Share certificate numbers (if kept in your possession).

Preparing additional information for your executor

This information should round out the above to provide a complete reference to your financial affairs. Include on it details about the following.

- Accountant's name, address, and telephone number
- Employment contract detailing employee benefits, the employer's telephone number, and the name and extension number of any individual in the company who handles benefits.
- Financial obligations, such as your mortgage and any other outstanding loans as well as any money owed to you.
- Investments – list them and the name and telephone number of your broker (who can provide information on short-term investments since it is difficult to keep an up-to-date record).
- Power of attorney – name, address and telephone number of those who have been given power of attorney and what the power covers (signing cheques, selling property, etc.).
- Properties owned, property locations and the whereabouts of the deeds.
- Safe-deposit box – its location, an inventory of its contents and where you keep the key.
- Whereabouts of:
  - personal papers;
  - bank records;
  - tax records.
- Will – its location and the name and telephone number of the solicitor who wrote it.

Maintaining the list

- You'll need three copies of your financial master list. One copy should be kept in your safe-deposit box; another should be in your Important Documents file; a third should be in your safe (see Chapter 21). Even if you've created it on the computer, make a print-out so that it will be available and accessible to those who need it.

■ Update the list as needed. Whenever you visit your safe-deposit box, check the contents against the list to make sure that it is up to date.

19

Investments

If you regularly pore over the financial pages checking the movement of your stocks and shares, then you probably have a system for watching your investments. Or perhaps you are more of a dabbler, or your great-aunt left you some shares, and now you need to become more knowledgeable. Whatever the case, you will benefit from using this basic system for tracking your portfolio.

While a paper-and-pencil system will always work, your investment life will change if you have access to the Internet or to online services. Keep reading to find out how you can benefit.

Establishing a system

- Gather together any material you have received from your stockbroker. This would include statements, as well as buying and selling confirmations. Because this information needs to be kept with your annual records, it will eventually be stored in the Investments section of your household affairs folder, but first you need to make a list of your holdings.

- Establish a separate sheet for each type of account you have – your own, joint or custodial.

- Here's the information you will need to record: name of the stock or bond, the number of shares/amount you own, date acquired, total cost of purchase including commission. When you sell, note the date sold and total sale price. You'll then want to note your profit or loss. Your charts might look like this:

CHART 1

Stock	No. of shares	Date acquired	Cost or other basis	Date sold	Sale proceeds	Profit/ loss

CHART 2

Bond	Amt. bonds	Date acquired	Cost or other basis	Date sold	Sale proceeds	Profit/ loss

- If any of your holdings are gifts or inheritances, you'll need to ascertain what date to use as your acquisition date and the amount that should be your cost basis. The executor of the estate or the person who gave you the gift can provide this information.

- Note that if you hold long-term bonds (for example, for your children's education), you should indicate the date they will come due. This will aid you in planning and organising for that time.

- If you participate in mutual funds, employee stock funds, or an investment club, you should keep track of those investments in a similar manner.

- All records of purchases and sales of the same security should be kept together.

- Save all the transaction confirmations you receive, and file them in your household affairs folder under Investments. They will be an important validation of your list.

Tracking income

- If the securities are income-producing, you will need to track these payments as well. Some people have the cheques sent to their homes; others have the income deposited directly into their accounts.

- To track income, set up a simple list that notes the name of the company, the amount of the dividend or interest payment, and the date. (When you buy or sell a bond there will be interest income or interest expense on the confirmation that should be included on this list.)

Stock/bond	Date	Dividend or interest received	Taxable	Non-taxable

- Keep this list in your Investment file in your filing cabinet since it is a permanent record you may refer to frequently.

Tracking performance

- Track the performance of your portfolio regularly. Financial advisers recommend doing it at least quarterly, if not monthly or more frequently.

Date	Stock/ bond	Original cost	Price now	% + or –	Action?

- To see how your investments are doing, note the date and the share price. Then compare your original investment cost with the current price to see whether you have a profit or loss. Also compare the current price with the price the last time you tracked performance to see how they compare. As you check each stock, make notes as to any action you might want to take. (Buy? Sell? Watch closely?)
- Check your investments regularly to make sure they are in line with your financial goals and are performing well for you.

Investment-watching made easy

If your home or office computer has access to online services or to the Internet, you're going to find that the work of tracking your investments has suddenly become easy.

Online services offer the capability of tracking your stocks for you, keeping you up to date (within 15 minutes) of the daily happenings of the stock market as well as your own portfolio. All you have to do is enter your stock name, the purchase price, and the number of shares you bought, and each time you click 'quote', you'll find out whether your stocks are up or down.

Online services and the Internet also offer a wealth of information to make you a more knowledgeable investor. You can find Web sites for individual companies or, through an online service, ask for an information sheet on a company in which you might invest. You'll find everything from global business news stories to minor, but helpful, details such as a listing for various companies and their 'ticker' symbols (how they are listed and in which market the stock is traded).

The interactive world has opened up countless opportunities for keeping current and learning more about investments. Once you have a taste of it, you'll never turn back.

20

Personal Property Inventory

If you were burgled or your house or flat destroyed by fire, would you be able to provide your insurance company with itemised receipts for your more valuable possessions? Most people would have to answer 'no'.

This chapter will provide you with a system so you will be able to say 'yes'. In addition to creating a record-keeping system for receipts, a Personal Property Inventory – which provides a record of your possessions – will help you get the full value from your property insurance should a disaster ever occur.

Taking an inventory

- You are going to need to take an inventory of your home, but before doing so, call your insurance agent to ascertain what type of information (and proof of possession) is required under your policy.

- Set aside time for this project. Some people prefer to devote a Sunday afternoon to it; others prefer to do it a room or two at a time. A simple room might take five minutes while a more complicated room might take up to an hour. Though the project may seem overwhelming, it will seem to go more quickly if you think of it room by room.

- Have on hand:
  - pen;
  - pad of paper (or ask your insurance agent to provide an inventory booklet);
  - camera with several rolls of film, or a video camera;

- a fire-resistant safe, available at most office supply stores. This is a sensible place for storing the inventory once you've finished it.

■ Choose a room in which to begin. Note down the major items you have there.

■ After each item note the year of purchase and the price. (If you don't know the exact price, you'll have to estimate.)

■ Your inventory list might look like this:

STUDY		
Item	*Year Purchased*	*Cost*
Colour TV/Sony	1995	£300
VCR/Sony	1994	£250
Sofa-bed/Heal's	1997	£1000

■ Next, take a photograph or videotape of each of the different sections of the room, showing as many items as possible.

■ Proceed to the next room, remembering to check the kitchen, bathrooms, and hallways for items of value.

■ Don't forget drawers. Check each one, and itemise and photograph valuables.

■ Items of particular value such as jewellery may need to be covered under a rider to your household insurance policy and will also need to be carefully documented.

■ Order two copies of the photos you need, or make copies of the videos. Arrange to have three copies made of the inventory. One set of photos or videos and an inventory will be stored in your home safe (preferably fire-resistant); another set and an inventory should be stored in your safe-deposit box; the third copy of the inventory should be kept in your Insurance file in the filing cabinet.

Updating the inventory

If you ever need to make an insurance claim, agents much prefer it if you can provide receipts for all the major possessions. Receipts are the key to the future maintenance of your Personal Property Inventory.

- For claim purposes, you need to decide what value constitutes a large purchase. You may want to check with your insurance agent.

- If you have not already done so (as suggested in Chapter 20), you will now need to create a list for these items. On a sheet of paper, write 'New purchases' and the year. File it in your cash receipts file.

- As you make purchases throughout the year, note those that are 'large' on this sheet; after you've paid the bill, take the receipt for each item and store it in an envelope along with your inventory list.

- On 1 January when you are packing away old household records to make way for new ones, transfer the past year's inventory list and the sales receipts to your safe.

- Create a new 'New purchases' sheet for the upcoming year. (Put a reminder slip 'Start new inventory sheet; move old one' in your January tickler file to make sure the job gets done.)

21

Safe-Deposit Box and Strong-Box

You may think you don't need a safe-deposit box. Your papers are 'fine where they are', and you have the perfect place for hiding your valuables ... Do you:

- Hide your money in a book?
- Keep money or jewellery in canisters or wrapped in tin foil in the refrigerator or freezer?
- Freeze small pieces of jewellery inside ice cubes?

One woman I know is so untrusting of institutions (and people) that she carries her entire savings – thousands of dollars – with her wherever she goes!

The problem with all of these methods is they are unreliable. The best place for important papers and valuables is in a safe-deposit box.

When it comes to having one, there are two main problems people encounter:

- They don't know what to keep in it. 'Should I keep the original of my will there? Do my insurance policies need to be stored in it?'
- They don't know a good system for keeping track of what is in the box. 'Is my passport there, and where is our marriage licence?' 'Did I put my gold fob watch in the box, or is it missing?'

This chapter will help you organise the contents of your safe-deposit box. You will never again need to worry about what you're keeping in it. We'll also talk about safes at home, and I'll list for you what should be kept there.

Selecting what goes in your safe-deposit box

Anything that is too valuable to be accidentally misplaced or destroyed by theft, fire or natural disaster should be stored in your safe-deposit box. Typical items include:

- certificates of birth, death, marriage and divorce;
- a copy of your will with a note specifying the location of the original – usually with your solicitor. Another copy should be kept in your filing cabinet;
- financial master list (see Chapter 18) for your executor noting the exact location of important documents; names and addresses of personal and legal advisers; (original in safe-deposit box; one copy in Important Documents in filing cabinet; another copy in your strong-box;)
- legal documents;
- mortgage papers;
- passports;
- pension plan;
- personal property inventory (one copy in safe-deposit box; one copy in file; one copy with receipts in strong-box);
- share certificates, bonds certificates;
- deeds of property;
- trust documents.
- In addition, you may choose to store small valuables such as jewellery or valuable collections such as coins and stamps here permanently or while you are on holiday.

Box maintenance

- Make a list describing all items in your safe-deposit box and keep it in your filing cabinet under Important Documents.
- Arrange the contents in the safe-deposit box neatly. Store the documents in clearly labelled envelopes.

- Not even safe-deposit boxes are 100 per cent safe. If the vault is robbed, banks generally do not have insurance covering the contents of safe-deposit boxes. If you are storing items of exceptional value, you may want to add a rider on your household insurance policy providing the coverage you need.

- Visit the box at least once a year to check the contents, and update your list as needed. (Put a reminder note in your tickler file.)

The need for a strong-box

A strong-box is a small fire-resistant file box that can be purchased at most office supply stores. Most strong-boxes will survive all but the most devastating fires, so they offer you a relatively safe place to keep important documents that don't really need to be in your safe-deposit box but would be inconvenient to lose in a fire or other natural disaster. Strong-boxes are not burglar-proof, so valuables should not be stored here.

Items you might keep in your strong-box include:

- financial master list;
- personal property inventory;
- new purchases sheets for each year along with receipts;
- all papers in your Important Documents and Insurance files that you would need in order to reconstruct your life after a fire or other property disaster.

Household Matters

22

In Case of Emergency

Whether it's a power failure or a serious injury, readiness is your best protection when there is an emergency.

Emergency procedures cards

Post an 'emergency procedures' card by all telephones and near the place you choose to keep your first-aid kit. The card should include the following information (type the names of the places and people in capital letters to make the card easy to read):

- The emergency telephone number for ambulance, fire brigade and police – 999.
- Address of nearest hospital casualty department and brief instructions on how to get there.
- Name and telephone number of family doctor; emergency number for out-of-hours calls.
- Telephone number of local police station.
- Address and telephone number of nearest chemist.
- Name and number of nearest neighbour who could help.
- Name and telephone number of family member (mother, brother) to call for help.
- Your own address, in case a flustered babysitter or cleaner is making the call. (In an emergency, even *you* might forget!)
- Name and telephone number of local vet.
- If there are children, the card should also include:
  - child's full name;
  - name, telephone number and address of child's doctor;

- parents' full names and work and mobile telephone numbers;
- child's blood type.

■ Family allergies, chronic illnesses (epilepsy, asthma, etc.), and any medications taken regularly that might affect emergency treatment

■ Make photocopies of the above information, and put them in accessible, logical places: one in the nappy bag, for example; one in the regular babysitter's wallet; a third in your Household Notebook (see Chapter 23). In addition, keep a supply of extra copies in a kitchen drawer. A new babysitter should be shown where the emergency numbers are posted and also instructed to take a photocopy from the drawer if he or she must leave with the children under emergency circumstances. The address of casualty, and your child's blood type, will be of little use if the sitter doesn't have the information with him or her.

Additional telephone numbers

In addition to the emergency numbers suggested above, you should also keep the following on hand in your Resource File (see Chapter 14) among your Home Service resource cards.

■ Telephone number of gas/electric company in case of power failure or gas leak.
■ Telephone number of appliance repair offices in case of malfunction.

Have on hand

■ Fire extinguisher.
■ Torch and batteries (check batteries periodically).
■ Candles and matches.
■ Tinned food.
■ Powdered or long-life milk.

- One good, easily readable book about first aid and emergency procedures. You may not have time to refer to it in an emergency, but if you do, it could make all the difference.

Courses everyone should take

Contact your local St. John's Ambulance or ask your doctor for information about the following:

- first-aid course, including instruction on CPR (cardio-pulmonary resuscitation) and mouth-to-mouth resuscitation;
- infant safety course.

For children

- When people other than their parents take your baby or child out of the house, you can help them to be ready for an emergency by preparing an envelope with the following information (print it on the outside of the envelope):
  - home, work and mobile telephone numbers; do not include addresses for security reasons;
  - telephone number and address of the child's doctor;
  - address of nearest casualty department.

- Put £20 in the envelope (usually enough to get a taxi to where they will need to go) and coins or a card for telephone calls. That way you've provided the information and the tools a person needs to cope with an emergency. The envelope should be kept in the nappy bag, for example, and pointed out to grandparents, babysitters, child-minders, and anyone else who might need it.

Teach your children

- As soon as possible (certainly by the age of three), begin training your child to dial 999. Very young children have been credited with saving the lives of others because they knew what to do in an emergency. Help them practise dialling so they'll be familiar with keying in numbers on the phone. Discuss possible scenarios with them in a matter-of-fact way: 'If I fell and hit my head and didn't get up, what would you do?' Their response should be that they would call 999 to get help.

■ Teach your children their telephone number and address.

23

General Household

Running a household requires excellent management skills – family scheduling, performing or delegating tasks, stock-taking and management, purchasing, budgeting, entertaining, and long-term planning (such as for a holiday or moving house) are all part of the job of a 'household manager'. The person responsible for seeing that everything gets done has as challenging a job as any manager in a business or corporation.

Establishing a notebook

To keep track of the many tasks, I recommend use of a special organisational tool, the 'household notebook'. You'll find that having all household-related information collected in one place is a real convenience.

- You're going to need a loose-leaf notebook, dividers (you may need as many as 10 or 12), and paper. The size of the notebook is up to you. Some people like to use a small, portable notebook so that they can carry it with them; others use a standard large format for home reference. Visit a stationery store and select the notebook that is right for you.

- The notebook is a perfect spot for lists of things, such as items to buy, to mend or to do, and people to call (see Chapter 39).

- Your notebook is also convenient for keeping track of housekeeping chores (see below), for emergency lists and numbers (see Chapter 22), and for party planning (see Chapter 34). In addition, the notebook can be as varied as it needs to be. Simply create categories as they become necessary. If you're redecorating, you may want to create a category for decorating ideas; you can even tape swatches of material and put paint samples there. If you're house-hunting, you can cut out and save property ads in it. You are sure to find it an invaluable aid in keeping track of a multitude of details.

General cleaning

Here are some suggestions for getting the housework done efficiently.

- Like anything else, housework goes better if there's a plan. Using your household notebook, set aside three pages for keeping track of housework. On the first, list jobs that need to be done daily; the second page should have items that need to be done weekly; the third should contain major tasks that can be done less frequently.

- Request help from other family members. (Refer to the chart or dial system in Chapter 50 for additional suggestions on distributing the chores.)

- Employ a cleaner on a regular basis. If you can't afford regular help, consider getting someone in to help with a specific task such as cleaning the attic, dusting all the bookshelves, and so on.

- Keeping up with the day-to-day tasks is vital. Most people find that doing one job each day is ultimately less time-consuming than an occasional full day spent cleaning everything:
  - if it's Monday, I do the washing;
  - if it's Tuesday, it must be vacuuming day;
  - if it's Wednesday, I need to grocery shop, etc.

- Before starting a task, decide how long you're going to spend on it. If you know that you can vacuum the house in 30 minutes, that's really not so bad.

- If you work away from home, save low-energy tasks for the evening. (One of my students got all her housework done during commercial breaks on television!) Try to do larger tasks on Saturday or before you leave in the morning. One working mother I know prepares the family dinner before leaving for the office in the morning.

- Do tasks in bulk. Don't iron one or two things at a time; wait until you have a week's worth to do. Just preparing for a chore like ironing takes long enough that you ought to maximise the 'setting up' time.

- Think of how to make chores more convenient. For example, an extension cord on your vacuum cleaner can greatly reduce the number of times you have to plug and unplug as you clean.

- Store cleaning supplies (furniture polish, window cleaner, spray cleaner, scouring powder) in a caddy and carry it with you as you clean. That way you're not always dashing back to the kitchen to get something you need.

- If you live in a two-level house, keep one set of supplies upstairs and one downstairs.

- When the time comes to deal with a major chore (cleaning out the attic, for example), one woman writes various tasks on several slips of paper and draws the 'chore for the day' out of the box. Whatever the slip says is what she will do.

- Organise your spring cleaning (the major tasks listed on page three of your household notebook housework chores) for set times throughout the year. For instance, once in March and again in September, send rugs and curtains out to be cleaned, have floors waxed, and loose covers changed. Set a time every other month to wipe out cabinets and bookshelves. Once it becomes routine, a matter of habit, it will get done automatically without your thinking twice about it.

Reducing clutter

- Leave an area as you found it (or better than you found it). If you've been watching some television, put back the magazines you thumbed through, and return the remote control to the drawer where it belongs. Don't leave anything out.

- Insist that family members help control clutter.

■ If doing away with the clutter seems too overwhelming right now, start with just one area, such as the front hall. Make it a point to put everything away as you arrive home and see what it's like to experience a clutter-free front hall. Once you've mastered a system for that area, move on to an area such as the dining room. You'll soon see that tackling just one area at a time will help make housework much simpler.

■ Whatever you do, don't tolerate 'messy clutter build-up'. It will multiply before your eyes! Control it before it gets out of hand.

24

Cupboards and Wardrobes

Clutter and chaos in cupboards! Most people suffer from it. How often have you resolved that 'as soon as I have the time, I'll clean out those cupboards'?

One day when I was visiting my aunt she asked me to help her reorganise her cupboards. When I said they looked great to me, she said, 'Oh well, I thought everything was supposed to be hung by length ...' I wish everyone was so well organised that 'hanging by length' was their greatest problem!

With a little thought – and some imagination – cupboard organisation can greatly simplify your life. The more organised the cupboard, the more you'll be able to put in it, and the easier the items will be to use. The following tips are designed to help you create your own personal system and to maximise your storage capacity.

Getting started

- Most cupboards can be reorganised in a day or less; however, in order to do it in that amount of time you need to have all the necessary supplies and organisers on hand. Read through the following information. Then devote a couple of hours to planning for your cupboard needs. After you've shopped for the necessary items, you can set aside half a day or so for each cupboard.

- Organisation begins with planning. Go to the cupboard and study its contents. Consider what should and should not be stored there. Should your tennis racket really be on the floor of your clothes cupboard? What about the humidifier? Isn't there a more logical place for it? Note down your space needs on paper.

Often it is not so much a matter of how much space you have as how successful you are at dealing with it.

■ Get specific measurements of everything (dresses, blouses, jackets, trousers, shoes, bags) to allow ample room for them. Measure the longest item in each category of items in determining the length of hanging space needed, and measure how much hanging space (in width) your clothing currently requires so that you'll have provided space for what you have. (Try to allow for 'breathing room,' too.)

Reorganising

■ Empty the entire cupboard. Weed out items as you go, throwing out or setting aside to donate what you don't want or haven't used in several years – if you haven't used it in that amount of time, you probably never will.

■ Clean the cupboard thoroughly. Vacuum the floor or the bottom, and wipe down the shelves. If you are repainting, use a high-gloss paint or polyurethane for easier cleaning in the future.

■ Measure everything carefully before installing adjustable, multi-level rods.

■ In homes with high ceilings, the upper reaches of a cupboard can often be fitted with a clothes rod, making a perfect spot for out-of-season storage.

■ Shelves should be adjustable and designed to serve individual requirements. When the shelves are very deep, consider sliding drawers instead.

■ Install a light that turns on when the cupboard door is opened.

Keep items visible and accessible

■ Categorise your clothes according to season, type and colour. Items that go together, such as trousers and jackets, should be kept together.

■ Store the clothes and shoes you wear most often within easiest reach.

- Invest in sturdy, well-made hangers. They'll help your clothes keep their shape longer and make it easier to stay organised. (Don't hang knitwear! Fold it with tissue paper instead.)

- Don't hang up clothes that need mending or cleaning. Establish a place to put them until they can be taken to the cleaner's or mender's. That way you'll know that all clothes that are hanging are ready to be worn. (Keep a list of what has been sent out; check off the item as it comes back.)

- Never store clothing in plastic bags. Plastic keeps clothes from 'breathing' and can cause discoloration. (Plastic bags are also a safety hazard if there are children in the home.) Instead, store clothes in cotton garment bags, preferably ones that are dark-coloured and won't permit light to come through.

- Use boxes for storage, but only if you can readily identify what is in them. The clear plastic boxes available in DIY stores are ideal, or you can label the box and list its contents.

- Most people store shoes on the floor of the cupboard, but it is better to keep the floor clutter-free. Otherwise, it becomes a sea of junk and collects dust; items stored there can get ruined. It's also one more area that will soon need cleaning out. Shoes should be stored in labelled (or plastic see-through) shoe-boxes, on shoe racks or on shelves.

- Hang hats and small bags on a board with hooks. You may want to use the board to decorate your room, and keep it outside the cupboard. Arrange the items in an attractive manner. This way of displaying your accessories will also come in handy when co-ordinating outfits or packing for a trip.

- Large handbags can be stored on shelves. (Hanging may cause large bags to droop and lose their shape.)

- Stuff hats and handbags with tissue paper to help them keep their shape.

- Belts and scarves can also be hung, or try rolling and placing them in conveniently located baskets or bins.

The linen cupboard

- In the linen cupboard, try rolling your towels, especially hand towels and flannels. You'll find this looks neater and saves space.

- When you store bed-linens and tablecloths, put the folded side out so that you take only the item you need. (If the edges are facing out, it's hard to determine how many sheets or towels you are removing.)

- Fold each bed-linen set as a unit (flat sheet or duvet cover and pillow cases within fitted sheet) so you pull out a single set each time. This also works well for sets of towels.

- Stack linens by room. Keep all sheets for the master bedroom together, all sheets for the guest room together, and so on. The same goes for towels.

- If your bathroom lacks adequate storage space, the linen cupboard is a perfect place to keep extra supplies of soap, tissues, toothpaste and lavatory paper.

The front hall

- Make sure the floor is clutter-free.
- Buy heavy-duty attractive coat hangers if there is a cupboard.
- Divide shelves into sections to organise hats, gloves and scarves; or use individual bins and baskets that are easy to reach. Large hats can be stored and protected in hat-boxes.
- If you have a great deal of storage up above, consider a curtain which draws across the shelf area to hide the clutter from guests.
- Put a mirror on the inside of the cupboard door for a last-minute peek at your appearance as you go out the door.

Re-designing

- Decide on the function of a particular cupboard. Will it be used for clothing or storage or linens?

- If you're building from scratch, decide exactly where the cupboard should go.
- Will you use doors, shelves, cupboards, pull-out drawers?
- Be specific about the amount of space you need and what you're storing.
- Size up your belongings. Measure everything to determine rod and shelf placement. Ten sweaters? Six bath towels? You need to allot proper space.
- Leave space for future purchases.
- Consider building compartmentalised drawers and shelves for dividing jewellery, belts and underwear. Pre-plan their arrangement by laying them out and drawing up a blueprint of the space. A carpenter (or you, if you're handy) can take it from there.
- Consider calling in a company that specialises in making cupboards. They often offer great advice and can arrange to do the design and building for you. Get prices from a couple of companies.

General

- Potpourri and sachets add a pleasing touch by scenting your cupboards. If needed, anti-moth sachets are also available.
- Remember to put things back where they belong. 'A place for everything and everything in its place' will put an end to the frustration of hunting for something and not being able to find it when it is most needed. Living by this rule will help simplify your life!

25

The Kitchen

When it comes to organising your kitchen, think about function, convenience and space. You need to consider how you use your kitchen. Are you primarily a baker? If so, creating a baking centre where all ingredients and appliances are within easy reach should be a specific goal. If you love to cook Chinese food, you'll want convenient cutting surfaces and clear work-top space near the stove.

Many of the suggestions apply to re-planning how to use your existing kitchen without major architectural work. However, if you are re-designing, simply use these ideas to help you formulate what your ideal kitchen should be.

Working with your plan

- Make a list of your specific needs. Note down the ideal areas you'd like to have – space for food preparation, room for baking – as well as your irritations – rubbish bin too far from main work area; pots and pans too far from the oven. If nothing comes to mind immediately, over the next few days note what works and what doesn't as you perform your usual tasks.

- If you are working with a designer, he or she should provide you with a plan for the layout as well as information on materials to be used and anticipated costs. While you'll want to give the designer the go-ahead once you are satisfied with the plan, remain flexible. Sometimes better solutions present themselves as the work moves along.

- Plan how you would like to arrange each area of the kitchen, one section at a time. Assemble the items that will need to be stored there. Before installing any of the suggested space-savers or making any structural changes, place the items in the cupboard and be certain the space is workable for what you have in mind. For example, if you put in cup hooks, will the shelf below be too cramped for the plates you planned to store there?

General rules

- Store items close to where they are used. Pots and pans should be located near the oven, glasses next to the sink or refrigerator, knives near the cutting board, and so on.

- Similar items (for example, all the equipment used for baking) should be stored together, except grocery items, which belong in the pantry.

- Frequently used items such as spices or coffee filters should be stored in the most accessible spots. Infrequently used items should be stored at the back of cabinets or up high, but not so far out of the way that you forget the item is there.

- Put away tinned foods by category. Label shelves for easy re-stocking. Alphabetise everything, including tinned foods and spices. It may seem compulsive, but finding things will become easier!

Cabinet storage

- The higher your ceiling, the higher you can go. Build cabinets up to the top of the room, and you will get a great deal of extra storage.

- When it comes to deciding where to place an item, consider how often you will need it. In general, remember that floor cabinets should be used for larger, less frequently used items such as pots and pans, while upper cabinets are generally used for glasses and dishes, which you may reach for several times a day.

- Kitchen shelves set at wide intervals are a waste of space when you are storing most things. For storing smaller items, divide the space by building half-shelves in between the larger ones (or you can buy adjustable shelving). If you build, have the shelves made so that they are adjustable. This way, they can be re-arranged according to your needs.

- Sliding shelves (or ones that swing out) can be installed easily and can bring forgotten pots and pans out into the open where they are easily accessible. A special rack will take care of lid storage.

- Have dividers built into a cabinet to store baking sheets, roasting pans and trays.

- Store baking tins by stacking in order of usage. If you rarely bake bread, put bread tins on the bottom.

- Make use of wire-coated shelf racks for organising dishes, cooking bowls, and the like.

- Mount hooks underneath a shelf inside a cabinet to hang cups up out of the way.

- For everyday use, have glasses and dishes that are stackable.

- If your glasses take up lots of cabinet space, try racks that fasten to cabinet walls or shelves and suspend the glasses from above, leaving enough room for plates, bowls, and so on, to be stored underneath.

- The back of a door in a cabinet or closet can provide convenient storage space in what would otherwise be wasted space. Several manufacturers make plastic-coated wire storage items, including baskets and grids with hooks and shelves, which can be used in many combinations and which attach to cabinet and door backs.

- You can also buy special organisers, which can be placed on the inside back of a cabinet door, for storing tin foil, waxed paper, cling-film and other such items.

- Under the sink, and on the inside of one cabinet door, attach the makings of a storage system for sponges, detergent, scouring powder, rubber gloves and cleaning brushes.

- Perhaps on the inside of the other door, place a rubbish bin with removable liners, or create a special cabinet with a bin for rubbish and another for recyclables.

- An awkward corner cabinet can be made accessible by using a spinning caddy, which can also be used for storing spices or small jars of baby food, for example.
- Customise your kitchen cabinets. Visit your hardware or DIY shop or the kitchen department of a department store and ask about the various kits available to extend kitchen space.

Drawers

- For organising the cutlery drawer, use a plastic tray. It keeps the drawer neat and slips out easily for cleaning.
- To keep a 'miscellaneous' (corkscrew, mixing spoons, spatula, etc.) drawer in order, use drawer dividers.
- Drawers are also a good spot for storing spices, tin foil, plastic wrap and food storage bags.
- Convert a drawer into a filing cabinet for recipes and warranties. If necessary, cut folders to fit.

Work-top space

Your main goal with work-tops is to keep them clutter-free. The following are some suggestions.

- Canisters and cookery books are frequently found on many kitchen work-tops. Find space for them on a handy shelf instead.
- Put away all appliances that aren't used daily. Mixers, blenders and most food processors should be stored in a cupboard rather than on the work-top.
- Some models of can opener can be mounted beneath the upper cabinet unit, leaving work-top space free for food preparation.
- Microwave ovens also take up work-top space. Certain ovens come with a microwave oven above; other styles of microwave can be mounted under the cabinet.

Creating extra work space

- If there is space available, consider buying or building a free-standing unit for the centre of the room. It adds more work space, and a shelf underneath can be used for large cookware.
- If you don't have space to add an additional work-top permanently, consider building one that flips up (or folds down or slides in) when not in use.
- Build a removable (or sliding) cutting board for the top of a drawer to extend your work area.
- A cutting board that fits across the sink also provides additional work space.

On-the-wall storage

- For frequently used items or for those for which you simply don't have the storage space, consider a wire grid unit on which pans and utensils can be hung from hooks. Cookware such as copper pots can be very decorative and the grid is functional as well.
- You can also hang cookware on a collapsible, stainless steel 'scissor' rack. The rack has hooks from which to hang the pots so that they are accessible but out of the way. When the 'scissor' mechanism is compressed the pots nest within each other, taking up very little space. When the rack is pulled out, the pots can easily be taken down from the rack. You may be able to find one of these racks in a hardware or DIY shop.
- Attach a wire basket to the wall under the top cabinet but above the work-top, to make a great storage spot for fresh fruit.
- A board with hooks can be a great addition to any kitchen. A large one can be used for storing pots and pans, or a smaller one placed above the work-top can be used with an easel attachment to hold a cookbook.
- Consider a wall-mounted grip in a cupboard for the mop and broom.

More ways to organise your kitchen

- Evaluate your electrical sockets. Are they well placed? If not, sockets can be added at a reasonable cost. Ask friends and neighbours to recommend a good electrician, or look in the Yellow Pages.

- Consider track lighting directed at work areas.

- For serious pastry-making, a piece of marble built into a work-top can make all the difference! Because it stays cool, rolling out the dough is much easier.

- Don't forget the ceiling! A rack suspended from it can provide an attractive and functional way to hang pots and pans.

- Certain commercial products, such as a free-standing metal shelving unit to store food, supplies, bowls, dishes, and so on, are durable and very functional. Visit a commercial supplier to see what would work for your kitchen.

- Plastic stacking-bin units (with or without wheels and usually consisting of three or four bins) can be a terrific spot to store place mats and ripening fruits and vegetables.

- Store cleaning supplies in a carrying caddy, which sits neatly in a cupboard, and can be easily moved around the house.

- Towel racks are sometimes a problem, but adhesive-backed ones can be put up conveniently near the sink; if you have an appliance near the sink, you might consider a magnetised one.

- Take advantage of new developments in ironing boards, depending on your space requirements and needs. I have seen one that comes as a complete ironing centre, with fold-out ironing board, an electric socket, a light and a place for storing the iron. It can be made to fit in flush with cabinets; or if placed against a wall, protrudes very little.

- When loading the dishwasher, group together items such as forks, spoons, knives, salad plates, glasses, and so on, to simplify putting them away.

■ Since the kitchen generally serves as the family communication centre, establish a message centre there. Prepare a chart like the following:

Mum	Dad	Amanda	Elizabeth	Julia

- Place telephone messages, notes and reminders here. This is also where you should hang the family wall diary so that all family members can jot down where they will be each day.
- Emergency information should also be posted near the telephone and family message centre (see Chapter 22).

26

The Refrigerator

Even a refrigerator needs to be managed. By doing so, you'll make meal preparation easier and cut down on wasted foods by using your leftovers efficiently.

Starting over

- Refrigerators need to be cleaned out and wiped down regularly. The best time to clean your refrigerator is when you are low on food.
- Empty the refrigerator one shelf at a time. Wipe down each shelf as you go.
- Throw away out-dated items, old cheese, half-used cans of tomato paste, opened jars of spaghetti sauce, jam you'll never use, and all the things that have been in your refrigerator too long or will never be used no matter how long they sit there.
- Don't forget to take out and evaluate items stored in the door. Door shelves should also be thoroughly cleaned.
- Empty the drawers and crisper. These drawers are generally removable so you can clean them more easily.
- Sort through freezer items. Remember that freezing just slows spoilage, it doesn't prevent it.

Storage tips

- Establish a purpose for each shelf – one for milk, juice and other drinks, one for meats, one for dairy products, and so on.
- Group together similar items.

- Put the items used most frequently near the front of the shelves; those used less frequently belong at the back.

- Date and label all home-wrapped items that go in the refrigerator or the freezer. You really won't remember!

- Eggs stay freshest if kept in their original carton.

- Milk and other dairy products should be stored on the coldest shelf, well inside the refrigerator.

- Store refrigerated meat on the coldest shelf.

- Cut up carrots and celery sticks as soon as possible after you buy them, and store them with a bit of water in a plastic container for easy snacking.

- Stack loaves of bread (dated and labelled) in the freezer. Slice any unsliced loaves, for easier thawing, and so that you can even thaw single slices as needed.

- Leftovers can be stored in stackable containers, preferably see-through, so you'll know exactly what you've got.

27

Supermarket Shopping

There are ways to accomplish your food shopping more efficiently. Try some of the following.

Establishing a system

- Plan all your meals at least one week in advance, and note what foods and ingredients you'll need to buy on your next shopping trip. You don't want to find yourself without tomato sauce if you were planning to make lasagne.
- Make and keep handy a list of ingredients for your most frequently prepared recipes.
- Plan to double up on cooking so you can freeze a complete dish for another night. Take this into account as you consider grocery needs.
- Choose a spot in the kitchen where you can conveniently keep your shopping list and a pen or pencil.
- On the list, record everything you need. If you don't write down each item as you think of it, you will eventually forget to pick up something you 'always' buy.
- Teach family members to record all of their grocery needs.
- Look out for a very small file in which to keep money-off vouchers, stored by category. Before going shopping, pull out the vouchers you know you'll use.
- This file is also the perfect place to store labels or a list of your favourite brands of certain products. (You may forget your favourite type of salad dressing.)

- Also prepare a list of details such as the different types of light-bulb you need. Keep the list in your file. You will find that the list is particularly helpful when taking advantage of special offers.

Shopping

- If you can, shop during periods of least activity, preferably when the supermarket is fully stocked. Monday morning can be a bad time for shopping because the new deliveries are arriving and the aisles are crowded with boxes as the staff try to re-stock the shelves after the weekend. Mid-morning or mid-afternoon can be a good time. You can ask the manager when the shop is not busy or experiment by going at different times.

- Buy in bulk or in economy sizes. Not only will you save money, but you'll be able to shop less frequently. Sometimes the butcher will give you a discount for buying an entire side of beef and let you take it home as needed.

- Take advantage of special offers. If tuna is priced at a discount, buy ten cans instead of one.

- Some people like to minimise the number of shopping trips they make by buying in bulk. You may get away with shopping only every other week or even once a month if, for example, you buy three boxes of the family's favourite cereal and a dozen rolls of paper towels. Having a freezer is a help, too.

At home

- Establish a pantry area (even if it has to be a cupboard outside the kitchen) for storing back-up items. Both on kitchen and pantry shelves, organise by categories (all tinned goods together, all baking supplies together, etc.).

- Once home, re-wrap meats in appropriate portions. Wrap some for individual-sized servings for occasions when you're cooking for only one person. Label and date them.

- When freezing, always label and date both new purchases and leftovers.

Other tips

- Whenever possible, order groceries and paper goods by phone.
- At smaller shops, such as the butcher's or the bakery, you can sometimes phone in your order in advance.
- Consider buying cleaning items from commercial suppliers. They are stronger, better and cheaper.

Stock control

- Keep a back-up supply of all items. When you reach the end of the sugar, for example, open up the extra bag and then add sugar to your next shopping list.
- Teach family members to be diligent about jotting down items when you are low – not when you've run out.

28

The Laundry

My sister has two sons and recently married a man who has a son of his own. I happened to be there the day they finished doing their first joint laundry. My sister simply looked in horror at a table with piles and piles of underpants, vests and at least two dozen pairs of dark socks. 'Ronni,' she said to me, 'there has got to be an organised way to do this.'

While most of us learn what we need to know about dark loads and light loads and washing towels separately when we first move away from our parents' home, no one gives much thought as to how doing the washing can be simplified or – in the case of a large family – better organised for speedier sorting.

Before you wash

Extra care before putting clothes into the washing machine will save you effort in the long run.

- Re-attach loose buttons and do any mending before the item is washed, and remove unwashable items such as belts, shoulder pads and any ornamentation.
- Turn clothing right-side out.
- Turn pockets inside-out and turn down the cuffs. Brush out sand, fluff and dirt.
- Close zips, fasten hooks, and button up for easier folding.
- To save on hand washing, use a lingerie bag for delicate underwear and stockings.
- Pre-treat stains or pre-soak badly soiled items.

Simplify

- To streamline doing the laundry, you want to do it as seldom as possible but often enough to keep everyone's drawers well stocked with clothing. Some people can wash just once a week; others must do it two, four, or six times a week.

- If there is really only one reason (say, fresh underwear) that makes frequent washes necessary, consider buying extras.

- Try doing hand washing in the shower. It makes perfect sense. During the minute or so you would normally luxuriate in the warm spray, you can rinse out a couple of items.

- When putting laundry away, group together items by the room in which they belong: stack them in the laundry basket in order of which room you will visit first (top) and which you will go to last (bottom).

Organising for the larger family

- As suggested throughout the book, colour-coding can be a real aid. Assigning each family member a colour can simplify the sorting of some items of clothing (children's pyjamas and underwear) as well as bath towels and flannels. For bedding, sheets can be easily identifiable by using different patterns for each bed so there's no confusion about what goes where.

- Have different laundry baskets for different members of the family. When you wash, do an entire load of only one person's clothes or combine the clothes of family members that are easily distinguishable from each other (Mum and oldest son, etc.).

- Use different coloured laundry pens for each family member to identify any similar belongings. Make a mark on the label large enough so that it is noticeable at a glance.

- Purchase an assortment of baskets to keep in the laundry room – one for each family member. Label and use it for that person's laundry. As soon as they are old enough, encourage your children to pick up their own basket and put their laundry away.

29

The Medicine Cabinet

Neglecting to organise your medicine cabinet can sometimes be dangerous. I'm sure you've heard stories of people who have got up in the middle of the night for an aspirin and have accidentally taken some other type of pill, or put nose-drops in their eye.

You should regularly take stock of your medicines, throw out what isn't needed, organise what is, and make a shopping list for first-aid supplies you really ought to have on hand.

Taking stock

- Spread out all items from your medicine cabinet.

- Old prescription medicines (unless they are for a chronic problem or a recurring ailment such as an allergy) should be thrown away – flush them down the toilet so that a child or pet won't retrieve them from a bin.

- Check expiry dates on all over-the-counter medicines; those that have expired should also be flushed down the toilet.

- Dispose of all over-the-counter medications whose exact use you don't remember and those you don't expect to need again.

- Age and exposure can cause medicines to change, so discard most items over a year old.

- Anything without a label should be thrown away.

- From this time on, label all medicines with the date of purchase and what it was for. (How often have you found an old tube of cream and can't remember whether it was for a cut or a rash?)

- All prescriptions should be labelled with the name of the medication, the date, the person's name and the instructions. If your chemist has not provided that information, add a label of your own.

Organising your medicines and supplies

- Wipe down the bathroom medicine cabinet. The items you keep here should be things you use daily – toothpaste, deodorant, comb, brush, razor. Because heat and damp make medicines age faster, the bathroom is not the best place to store medications.

- Select and clear out another space where you can store your medicines and first-aid supplies. Be sure the space is well lit so you will not mistake one medicine for another. If you have children in the household, select an inaccessible cabinet that can be locked.

- Before you start putting things away, establish categories of items and label shelves in the bathroom and in the place you've chosen to keep medicines accordingly ('Hair care', 'Skin care', 'Daily medicine'). You'll be able to find things much more quickly and easily – and it will be much more difficult to mistake the nose-drops for eye-drops because you'll have two different spots for them.

- Buy a first-aid box so that all emergency supplies can be kept handy in one place.

- Clean out your medicines annually, throwing out anything you haven't used in the past year. Re-stock on first-aid items you might need.

Safety tips

- If you have children, buy bottles with child-proof caps, but keep in mind that 'child-resistant' does not mean it's truly tamper-proof.

- Keep all medicines in their original containers to avoid having someone mistake one medicine for another.

- Read all labels carefully and administer exactly as directed. At night, turn on a light to make sure you have the right medicine and to see that you are measuring accurately.
- After using a medicine, re-cap it immediately.
- Always return supplies to storage immediately after use.
- Before purchasing over-the-counter items, ask your doctor for recommendations.

First-aid supplies to have on hand

- Antibiotic ointment or spray to prevent infections in cuts
- Antiseptic
- Assorted plasters, bandages, a sterile roll of gauze with adhesive tape and scissors to cut tape
- Burn ointment or spray
- Calamine lotion for bites and minor rashes
- Elastic bandage
- Epsom salts
- Eyewash and cup
- Heating pad
- Insect repellent
- Thermometer
- Sterile cotton
- Sunscreen
- Tweezers
- Vaseline

Basic over-the-counter medicines to have on hand

- Antacid
- Anti-diarrhoea medicine
- Anti-histamines for allergic reactions

- Aspirin or Paracetamol
- Nasal spray
- Oral decongestant

30

Taking on Household Help

The best way to approach this task is to go about it in a business-like manner and then do all you can to maintain a good relationship.

Defining the job

Before you go about looking for the perfect person to solve your problems, you need to make some decisions.

- Think through the job carefully. Decide which hours you will want someone.
- List the duties to be performed.
- Make a list of the qualities and skills you'd like this person to have. Ironing skills? Ability to follow a recipe? Kind and loving with children? Likes pets?
- Will this person travel with you on business or on holiday?
- Talk to friends and relatives about salary, benefits, and holidays, and decide what you want to offer.
- Decide whether you need the person to drive.
- Decide whether you mind if a person smokes.

Starting the search

- Referrals are the best way to find good help. Ask friends and family to keep their ears open. You may hear about a friend of a friend who is looking for work.
- Contact agencies.
- Put ads in newspapers. Spend enough money on an ad so you can be very specific about your needs (time availability, non-

smoker, driver's licence, etc.). That way the majority of calls you get will be from people who meet those criteria.

■ Watch for notices on bulletin boards at the doctor's surgery, children's shops, nursery schools or child care centres, or put up a notice yourself.

Pre-screening

Especially if you've run an ad, you're going to need a method for deciding which of the callers you want to see in person.

■ Make up a questionnaire and photocopy it, leaving copies by each telephone with a pen or pencil. The form should have space for the person's name and telephone number, previous employment, your general feeling about him or her ('sounds cheerful', 'English not terrific'), and any point you specifically care about (non-smoker, likes pets, willing to travel with you and baby if necessary, will work overtime). Try to clarify by phone whether the person fits your basic needs.

■ Look for good language skills (at least good enough to communicate with you), general enthusiasm for the job, and a positive attitude. In the conversation you should:

 • re-emphasise the days and hours of the job. Ask about the person's availability during those times;

 • go over job responsibilities and the necessary skills;

 • ask about the person's most recent job. Why is he or she leaving?

■ Describe where you live and ask how the person plans to get there.

■ If you have a positive feeling based on this short conversation, arrange an interview. Or you may prefer to take the person's name and number until you decide on the top three people you want to see. When you set up the appointments, make sure you do the following:

 • emphasise that it's very important they phone if they can't make it.

- be sure to get their telephone number so you can call and cancel if you need to. Or ask them to call you in advance of the appointment so that you both can confirm;
- give them precise directions to your home.

The interview

Most people are very nervous at interviews, so don't discount them immediately just because they seem ill at ease. Begin by again describing the job so they have time to collect their thoughts. During the course of the interview, you will want to ask the following questions.

- Where did you grow up?
- Are you currently employed, and if so, what kind of work are you doing? How long have you been employed there?
- Why are you dissatisfied with your current job?
- What tasks did you do at your last job?
- What other responsibilities or commitments do you have? (Here you're looking for whether they may have to take their mother to the doctor once a week or anything that might mean they would have difficulty getting to the job regularly.)
- What don't you consider part of the job?
- Are there any special things (bad back, dislike of pets, allergies) I ought to know about you?
- Put together some 'What if' questions to get a sense of how he or she would handle certain situations. If you're hiring someone to care for your elderly mother, ask questions like, 'What if my mother fell but refused to let you take her to the doctor?' Or for a babysitter: 'How would you discipline my child if he ran out into the street before you said it was time to cross?' Or: 'What would you do if there were lots of laundry to be done, but the baby cried every time you put her down?'
- Are you willing to follow a checklist of daily tasks? (Show him or her one.)

- If he or she is to live in, show the person the room where he or she would sleep.
- Check the candidate's eligibility to work in your country. Ask for current references.
- If the person is foreign, you might ask if he or she has plans to return home soon. (There's little sense in training someone who won't be around for very long.)
- Be sure to specify days off, pay, holidays and benefits.
- If the person is to care for children or the elderly, leave him or her alone with them for a little while. You can wander in and out of the room or eavesdrop to get a sense of how the person handles things. Trust your gut feelings.
- If the person is to drive, check their driving licence.

Checking references

Do call the references. Ask the following questions.

- How long has he/she been with you?
- Why did he/she leave?
- How well did he/she follow instructions?
- Could he/she think quickly in an emergency?
- Was he/she responsible, and did he/she use common sense?
- How well did he/she get along with family members? Was he/she chatty or quiet?
- For child care, how did he/she spend time with your child(ren)? Was he/she particularly good with one age or another? With one type of activity or another? Did your child(ren) like him/her?
- Is there anything important I should know about him/her – positive or negative?
- Was he/she punctual?
- Do you have any advice for us in working with him/her?
- Would you employ this person again?

Working together

- Once the person has agreed to work for you, review again the pay, holiday, benefits, system of raises, and sick leave arrangements, and set up a probationary period.

- Establish exactly what the job is. Discuss any peculiarities of yours, such as 'I can't stand to find dishes left in the sink'. Or, 'Please make sure the baby's room is tidied up before you leave.'

- Discuss expectations, hours, punctuality and the use of your phone and television.

- Show the person the appliances and how they operate. (If necessary, compile a manual for them.)

- Specify items not to be touched or cleaned.

- Ask him or her about foods he or she likes and any special dietary needs.

- Buy any needed items if the employee is to live in.

- Write out instructions and set up tasks to be done daily, weekly and every two weeks.

- Check their tax and National Insurance situation.

- Keep accurate records of sick days and holidays.

- Just as you expect your worker to be punctual, you should be as well. If you've said you'll be home at six o'clock, you should be there 99 per cent of the time.

- Keep the relationship professional. Mild interest in your employee's personal life is fine; don't try to become his or her best friend.

Additional tips for working with a child-minder or babysitter

- Discuss child-rearing practices.

- Establish a regular time each week when you can discuss how things are going. Perhaps you can come home 15 minutes early (or leave the house a little later) one day a week.

- Keep in mind that your child's needs will change and what used to be a two-hour nap may now have shrunk to one hour. Realise that your employee may need some decrease in his or her other responsibilities because of that.
- Ask neighbours to keep an eye out, and occasionally come home earlier than usual just to see how things are going.

Main Events

31

Preparing for the Painters

Some people say that having your house or flat painted is worse than moving, and they may be right. Certainly, having to pack up all your belongings and pile them in the centre of a room is a time-consuming process. However, if you can keep in mind how beautiful a new colour scheme and a freshly painted room will look, the nuisance of having to prepare for it won't seem as bad.

Choosing a painter

- Get recommendations from friends. Ask to see the person's work, if at all possible.
- Get prices from at least three painters.
- Ask prospective painters the following questions.
  - Who will actually be doing the work? The painter? An assistant? Will he or she be there throughout the job?
  - How will the walls be prepared?
  - Who will order and pick up the paint?
  - Is paint included in the price?
- Show the painter the space that is to be painted, asking if he or she foresees any problems.
- Make sure the person has the proper insurance.
- Check with previous clients as to whether or not the person stayed on schedule, stuck to the stated price, and was pleasant to have around.
- Once you've selected a painter, go over everything step by step. Make sure the person cleans up each night so you can still live in your home.

- Prepare a room-by-room checklist before the job begins. (How will the painter protect door-knobs and light-switches? Should you remove them? Or will the painter?)
- If carpets will be laid afterwards, make an agreement for the painter to come back to do touch-ups.
- Work out a pay schedule consisting of a deposit and payment of the balance. Some workers request a mid-point payment, but specifying what is 'half-way' can pose a problem.
- Draw up a written agreement that is very specific.

Choosing a colour

- Collect swatches of wallpaper and fabric to take to the paint shop.
- Initially, shop for a general colour without worrying about the exact shade. At the paint shop, you can pick up a wide variety of paint samples to avoid having to return again and again.
- Once you've selected the basic colour, buy a small quantity of that shade, and two others – one shade lighter and one shade darker. When you get home, paint test patches in the room on different walls in order to see the different colours in various lights.
- For high-traffic areas (particularly if you have children) consider a finish that is easy to wipe clean, such as a gloss.
- If you're responsible for buying the paint, ask the painter how much you will need.
- If the painter picks up the paint, be sure he or she does a test patch for colour.
- Label paint cans according to room.
- Keep a record of the paint used for each room. Note the colour, formula, brand and finish. File this information in your filing cabinet or in your household notebook (see Chapter 23).

Preparing for the painters

- Buy lots of dust-sheets to cover the furniture. You'll need tape, too.

- If cupboards are to be painted, clean them out. Borrow clothes-rails (ask friends and neighbours), and gather boxes (from supermarkets and off-licences) for temporary storage. If the cupboards don't need to be painted, take a plastic sheet and cover all the clothing within. Even when the door is closed, dust from preliminary sanding will get in.

- As you go through your cupboards, pull out items you no longer want. Give them to charity or throw them away.

- Send out rugs and curtains to be cleaned.

- Protect hardware. If the painter is not going to remove it, you should put each unit (one switch-plate and accompanying screws) in a plastic bag and label it. Keep all hardware and decorative switch-plates together in a box to avoid hunting for them later.

- Put the furniture in the middle of the room, cover completely with dust-sheets, and tape them down to the floor.

- If the paint job is complicated, draw a plan and code it. Put numbers on the wall and label each paint can accordingly. This lessens the chance of error.

- Have the living room done first. It's usually the largest room and when it's finished, you can store things from other rooms there while they are being painted. However, be careful not to mark or scratch the newly painted walls!

- Plan projects to do at home during the time you'll have to be there to supervise.

- Keep available all the things you'll need (appointments diary, outfit for the next day) so you won't have to dig for them.

- Make alternative meal plans for the period when the kitchen is being painted. A toaster, hot plate and electric kettle will allow you to prepare simple meals. You can request that you still have access to the refrigerator.

32

Moving

Whether it is across the country or just next door, moving house is a major undertaking that requires a great deal of planning and hard work.

People suffer from various moving miseries: some are still knee-deep in boxes months after a move is over; others never do unpack some of the things they moved with; others intend to unpack efficiently, but become overwhelmed when faced with a new living room full of boxes marked 'Miscellaneous'. I've never heard anyone say, 'I loved moving and can't wait to do it again!'

Moving should not be thought of as one major task, but many small tasks instead. Use this chapter and check off each task as you accomplish it; you'll soon see that by breaking down the move into parts, it can be managed and it *will* happen.

Sharing the news with your family

- Tell your children about the move early enough to let them adjust to the idea. As a general guide, children ages eight and over should be told early, probably as soon as you know. With children ages four to eight, give two to three months' notice; children under four should hear the news about a month ahead of time.

- On each child's level, explain why you're moving: 'Daddy's new job is in this town', or 'We'll be closer to Grandma', etc.

- Tell children what moving will mean to them: 'We're moving to a new house, but you'll still go to the same school . . .' 'When we move to Newcastle, we'll take all your toys, your furniture, and you, and in our new house, you'll have a room of your own.' Bring the subject up regularly so that it can be re-explained. Pre-school children may wonder exactly what gets packed, and some fear they will be forgotten in the shuffle, so always address how he or she will make the move, too.

- Young children don't understand time references such as 'next month', so give them a reference such as 'after you break up from school'.

- Find one or two features of the new area that you know each child will like. For a toddler it may be a terrific playground; for your 11-year-old son, it may be the football team for which he'll be eligible. If you can stress what will be new and special, it will help the children anticipate the move positively.

- Ask your librarian to recommend age-appropriate books on moving.

- If you're showing your house to prospective buyers, it's ideal if the children can be out of the house during appointments. The house will show better without chaos, but more important, the children won't have to focus on the fact that soon 'their' house will belong to someone else.

- When to move? Mid- or late August can be good; if the move is totally at your discretion, and you have children, between schools is the best. The summer provides a natural break in the year, and it is generally easier for children to adjust when they can get absorbed by a new school programme, meet new friends, and begin to learn the ropes along with other new children. If you have to move earlier in the summer, enrol your children in some type of regular activity (swimming, tennis or dance lessons) so that they can begin to meet other children right away.

Things to do as far in advance as possible

- Get recommendations about removal companies or check the Yellow Pages. Get two or three to come to your home for an estimate. Before they arrive, you'll want to have a general idea of what goes and what stays. If an entire suite is to be given away, you won't want the cost of moving it calculated into the overall estimate.

- When the removal company arrives, find out the following:
  - estimated moving costs;
  - how they will pack fragile items;
  - provisions of the contract;
  - insurance coverage (which you may need to supplement);
  - who will handle the move at the other end if you're moving to a place where the removal company doesn't have an office.

- Ask them if they will help you disconnect the washing machine and dryer, oven, refrigerator, freezer and television set. You'll want to know now if you need to make other arrangements.

- Carefully read the contract that outlines the terms of your move.

- Consider what work could be done in your new home before your arrival. You can probably arrange with the owners for a builder to make a visit there. If the place will be vacant for a few days or weeks before you arrive, you may be able to get some construction out of the way. Consider, too, whether a cleaning team, or window cleaner should come in before you arrive.

- You don't want to move what you don't want, so start taking stock of all your belongings. Sort everything into four groups:
  - items to throw out (don't insist that your children throw things out, as this will only make the move more difficult);
  - items to give to charity;
  - items to give to friends or relatives;
  - items to go with you.

- Start collecting packing materials. Your local off-licence may be a good source of boxes, or buy collapsible boxes from the removal company. They are strong, have tops, and can be used for storage (or stored flat) after the move. You'll also need tape. Newspaper makes the best packing material but can leave marks on your belongings.

If you are moving to a new area

- Write to the local Council or Tourist Information Office for information on the town. School-age children may want to write the letters themselves.

- Get hold of copies of the local newspaper to get a sense of the local news and the events for children.

- Research nursery schools and activities for older children before moving; you may need to pre-register. How to research? The estate agent may be able to put you in contact with other families who have moved to the area recently. Ask them about local Scout troops, football teams, extra-curricular activities, etc. Also inquire about babysitters. There may be one service everyone uses; they may know of someone who is looking for a job.

- Take the children to visit the new house and surrounding area as often as possible. Find the pizza places and where you can rent videos, visit the park, and so on.

- If the children can't come with you to visit, bring back printed information, and take lots of photos of things that will interest them. Put together a photo essay of where your family is moving, using pictures of the park, the swings at school, the ice rink, the pool, your new garden, etc. Younger children will love taking it to school to share with classmates, and it may make them feel more confident about going somewhere new.

Things to do four weeks in advance

- Begin sorting through your post to make a list of people to notify regarding your change of address – magazines to which you subscribe, credit card companies, department stores where you have store cards, and so on. Most can be notified by filling in the change-of-address section of a regular bill or statement. Notify all other companies and individuals by letter (photocopies of a standard letter will be fine), or use standard change-of-address cards. On your list, note the date you notified each person or company. (At a later date, notify the post office about forwarding your post.)

■ Confirm packing and moving dates.

■ Begin to use up food from the refrigerator and freezer, and only re-stock what you'll need during the next month.

Things to do four weeks in advance of a long-distance move

■ Make whatever travel plans are necessary. Do you need train or even plane tickets? Will you need to stay in a hotel the night after your old house is packed up? Will you need hotel reservations in your new town?

■ Make travel arrangements for pets. Ask your vet about tranquillisers, and make sure all vaccination papers are in order.

■ Notify schools.

■ Request recent x-rays (both dental and medical), and contact doctors and dentists to ask them for personal recommendations in your new area.

■ Make inquiries about a place of worship where you're going.

■ Return everything you've borrowed (including library books), and collect what you've lent.

Four weeks in advance: packing tips

■ Start packing items you're not using regularly such as good china, out-of-season clothing, and the contents of your attic or cellar.

■ Clean items before packing to save time when unpacking.

■ If possible, send carpets or rugs, curtains and duvets to be cleaned and have them delivered to the new address. Keep a list of what you send out so that you can be certain everything comes back.

- Keep things that belong together in the same cardboard box: pans with their lids, stationery with envelopes, remote control with the television.
- Fill all boxes to the top so that items won't move around.
- Try to distribute the weight evenly within each cardboard box.
- Use sheets, towels and blankets to cushion the contents of the boxes.
- Arrange to take house plants with you, as removal companies will generally not be responsible for them. Otherwise, give them away.
- Pack books flat so their spines don't break, and put them in smaller cardboard boxes so they won't be too heavy. Add additional packing material to empty corners so the books won't slide around. Books that will be shelved together should be packed in the same box.
- When packing lamps, remove bulbs before wrapping the base in a towel or blanket. Shades can be nested inside one another and packed in a separate box. Use packing material (not newspaper) to fill in extra space.
- Don't add heavy linens to drawers in furniture. Leave chests of drawers and desks with their normal contents.
- Consider asking the removal company to pack kitchen and fragile items. (Some will not take responsibility for items they have not packed.) Otherwise, fragile items and all dishes should be individually wrapped using newspaper or paper towels. Cushion them well.
- Leave rugs, pictures and mirrors in place. The removals men are best prepared to pack and wrap these.
- For hanging clothes you can sometimes buy cardboard 'wardrobes' from the removal company. Invest in these so that you don't have to pack your clothes.
- Fold curtains, bed- and table-linens so they can be draped over a hanger. Then they, too, can be moved in a cardboard 'wardrobe'.

- Provide each child with a box for their own special treasures. If driving to your new home, consider taking these boxes with you. If that is impossible, label them 'load last, unload first'.

- Establish a box for those items you will need throughout the move, and for valuables: plane tickets, driving itinerary, important papers, keys to the new house, jewellery, and so on. Keep the box handy so you can add to it as needed.

- In another box labelled 'load last, unload first', put clean bed-linens and towels so they will be accessible as quickly as possible once the truck arrives at your new home.

- Put together a survival kit with a hammer and screwdriver, tape, scissors, light-bulbs, a first-aid kit (including children's and adult pain reliever, plasters, antiseptic, tweezers, clean needle, cold tablets, and medicine for an upset stomach), paper plates, cups and napkins, plastic tableware, a small saucepan, instant coffee or tea bags, snack food, a can opener, paper towels, lavatory paper, detergent, sponges, plastic rubbish bags, and flannels.

- Number each box, and then label it as to its contents and the room where it will go. Also note the information on a separate sheet of paper; if you discover that box 33 is missing, you'll automatically know it had living-room lamps in it.

- Dispose of all flammables, such as cleaning fluid, paint and aerosol cans. The removals company will not take these things.

Things to do two to three weeks in advance

- If you're driving to your new house, have the car tuned up for the trip. Check the oil, water, battery and tyres.

- Call charities to pick up your donations, or deliver them yourself.

- Deliver or have picked up the items you plan to give to friends.

- Notify all utility companies of your departure, and arrange disconnection, if appropriate, for just after your departure; instruct the companies to send the final bill to your new address. Contact:

- gas/electricity companies;
- water supplier;
- telephone company;
- cable television company.

■ Notify the above utilities of the date you'd like service to start in the new location. (Have the telephone connected at least one day before the removal van's arrival.)

■ Call your insurance agent for policy changes, and discuss any special coverage that might be necessary during the move.

■ Arrange for the plumber or the appropriate service to install your appliances in your new house.

Things to do one week in advance

■ Pick up any items you might still have at the dry cleaners, laundry or anything that is being repaired.

■ If you're moving to a new area, go to the bank to sort out the following:

- ask them to transfer your account or arrange for a letter of credit to make it easy for you to set up a new account;
- ask them to transfer the contents of your safe-deposit box, or withdraw the contents of the box yourself and get the box released;
- withdraw sufficient funds to cover your expenses until you reach your destination.

■ Arrange for the forwarding of mail by the post office by filling and handing in the standard form.

■ Send change of address cards to your friends, including your new telephone number.

■ Arrange for child care. While it's a good idea for children to be at home on moving day, make someone else responsible for their well-being.

- For a long-distance move, pack suitcases with the clothing and items you'll need during the move.
- Mark 'Do not move' on all items you plan to carry with you.

Two days before

- Tape shut the tops of bottles and spillable items.
- Remove window fittings (curtains and poles) and take down special light fixtures not included in the sale of your house that you plan to take with you.
- Don't pack perishable items.
- Type out directions to your new house for the removal company.

Day before (packing day)

- When the removal men arrive to pack any items you've requested, point out fragile items as well as items not to be moved.
- As they pack, work with them by quickly checking the contents of each packed box. Label it according to its new location (main bedroom, kitchen, cellar, etc.) and its contents. Number each box and add it to your list of boxes and their contents. This will make unloading easier.
- Finish packing personal items.
- Make a final inspection of the house to check for details that need to be sorted out before the next day.
- Plan a simple breakfast for the next morning that can be eaten on paper plates.

Moving day

- Strip the beds, but leave the bottom sheets on mattresses and the bed assembled.
- Have the vacuum handy to leave the place in good condition for the new owner.

■ Include your children in the day's activities. Let them see that all their treasures are being packed with the rest of the household belongings. Ask if they can visit the back of the van to check that everything is going.

■ To avoid disputes later, accompany the removals people during the compiling of the inventory of goods to be moved.

■ Make a final tour of the house to be sure you have everything. Don't forget the vacuum cleaner!

■ Check, sign and save a copy of the bill of lading. Verify the address of your new home and the phone number of the person to be called if there are problems on the way.

■ Give the driver directions to the new address.

■ Confirm delivery date and time.

■ Leave keys with the estate agent, the new occupant or a neighbour.

■ Make sure all the windows and doors are closed and locked. Turn out all the lights.

■ Check with the removal company regarding final cost (determined on long-distance moves after the van is weighed). Make sure you'll have the right amount of money at your destination, as payment is often required before unloading.

Delivery day

■ Be on hand to show the removal people where things go.

■ Do not sign delivery papers until you've checked the inventory and inspected for damage. If any loss or damage is noted, ask the driver to make specific notes of loss or damage on the inventory list.

■ If it's necessary to claim for damaged or missing items, notify the removal company as soon as possible. They will send you claim forms.

After arrival: getting settled in your new area

- Shortly after arrival, take the family on a walk or drive around the area.

- Find out about local transport; get bus and train schedules, and appropriate maps.

- Contact the DVLC to change the address on your driving licence, and arrange for change of address on any other official papers.

- Research the new emergency numbers you'll need. Find out the location of the nearest hospital, casualty department and police station.

- Enrol your children in school, and visit the school to get them settled. Help them with ideas for getting to know new people.

- Arrange for a friend or new neighbour to keep an extra set of house and car keys.

- Make sure you are registered to vote in your new area.

- Find out about and sign up for some activities (to do separately or together as a family) that would help you meet some local people.

- Visit the library and apply for a library card.

33
Job Search

It's often been said that getting a new job is a job in itself, which is why organisation is so important. If you're still working, you need a very organised method for pursuing leads and following up during the time you can spare for the job hunt. If you're currently unemployed, setting up a system for your job hunt will keep you from becoming depressed, as you treat it like the nine-to-five job it should be.

Organising your job search

- Buy a loose-leaf notebook, dividers with pockets, and paper, or keep records of your search on the computer. You will need to divide it into the following sections:
  - Career goal. This section is for recording your thoughts (and final decision) regarding what type of job you are currently looking for (or could do). Long-term career planning ideas should also be a part of this section.
  - Contacts. In this section, list all the people whom you should contact to help you with your search. Also note down names of helpful organisations and target companies (those likely to have the type of job you are seeking).
  - Letters sent. File copies of all the letters you send out here. On the back of the letters, you can keep notes regarding subsequent conversations and meetings.
  - Interview preparations. This section will include a list of general questions for which you will want to be prepared, as well as notes, brochures, annual reports, and other information regarding specific companies.

- Follow-up. Keep a thank-you note list and tick it off after you've written to someone. Once you have been interviewed at a company, letters and related material should be moved here. This will provide an organised method for following up.

■ Buy high-quality paper for your letters.

■ Get an answering machine and record a pleasant, business-like message on it.

Identifying your goal

Be as specific as possible in setting a job goal. Use your notebook to record your thoughts. Take a long weekend or even a full week to consider exactly what type of job you're looking for (or could do). You may even want to visit a career counsellor for help in this area. Are you looking for exactly the same position you've had, only in a different or larger environment? Are you looking for a specific job in a field related to yours? Are you seeking a career change?

■ Now identify your target companies. You may already have some in mind, or your local library will have directories of firms in various industries. Ask the librarian for help.

■ Consider salary expectations. This will probably involve some personal research. Find out what the going rate is in the field. If you're very experienced, you can probably ask for more. If you're a novice, you should expect less.

■ Set goals regarding the number of letters to be sent and contacts to be made each week. The number you establish will depend on whether this is a full- or a part-time effort.

Preparing your CV

■ Prepare your CV on computer. This will make it easy to edit the CV frequently, and you'll also be able to provide pristine copies as needed.

- Tailor your CV to the type of job you are seeking. You may need to write more than one.

- Your CV should be no longer than two sides. Remember, it's the places where you've worked and your education that get you the interview, so sacrifice other information if you are short of space.

- Describe your jobs using active verbs, emphasising responsibilities and accomplishments: 'increased profits . . .' 'planned and executed programme . . .' 'supervised staff of 30. . .'

- Go over your CV's layout and content with someone whose business judgement you trust.

- Proof-read your CV carefully. There's nothing worse than a prospective employer finding a typographical error.

- If you provide the names of references on your CV, let them know that they may be contacted.

Preparing your covering letter

- Your covering letter is the gift-wrapping for your CV. It should help make your CV stand out from the others.

- Prepare a good basic letter. This will ensure against writer's block each time you send out your CV. Keep in mind that you will revise your letter each time, making it specific to the job and to the person to whom you are writing.

- Make the letter brief and to the point. Its content should focus on how you can help the company, not on how the company can help you.

Starting your search

- Turn to the Contacts section of your notebook and begin to note down all the people who might help you find a job: family members, friends, business associates, acquaintances. Because 70 per cent of all jobs are found through personal contacts, such people are very important.

- Also note down recruitment agencies and placement officers (such as your college placement officer), and, in the case of redundancy, any help offered by your employer. Cut out newspaper and trade magazine job ads that sound interesting.

- Keep up with trade journals and the business section of your local newspaper. Cut out articles about people or companies that interest you. Someone in the know who is smart enough to follow up on an article may well get a job interview!

- You can also obtain new contacts by attending meetings, lectures, and seminars, and trade fairs.

- Once you have a list of names, begin looking up addresses and telephone numbers. You may need to call the company for the person's exact title, the correct spelling of his or her name, telephone extension.

- Be sure to list target companies for whom you would like to work. If you don't have an inside contact there, call and get the name of the person responsible for recruitment in the division that interests you.

- Since your basic covering letter and CV are now prepared, you can immediately begin to approach the people you've listed on your Contacts page. In many cases, your goal is simply to be referred to someone who might have a job opening, so your covering letter should state that and note that you will follow up with a phone call.

- Photocopy each letter you send out, and file it in the 'Letters sent' section.

- Once the letters have been sent, use your diary to note the days on which you need to follow up.

- When you phone the person (as you must do with every letter you send), keep notes regarding your conversation on the back of the covering letter. Note down the date of the conversation and any referrals, and make sure you get the name of the secretary or PA . That person is the key to your getting through again if you need to.

- Any referrals you are given should be added to your Contacts list. Make sure you note by whom you were referred.

Prepare yourself before each interview

- Do some research about the company. If possible, talk to people who work there or who know others who do; try to locate and read any printed material about the company.
- Acquaint yourself with the company's product(s), if applicable.
- Think through the position for which you're applying, and note down any questions you'll want to ask. For example, you'll want to learn how the position works, what the responsibilities are, how much travel must be done, and where you would fit into the hierarchy. These questions should be filed in the 'Interview preparations' section of your notebook for handy reference.
- With the specific company and job in mind, consider any special questions the interviewer may ask.
- Ask someone to help you rehearse.
- Prepare an answer to the standard line: 'Tell me about yourself.' Don't be afraid to sell yourself. I once went on an interview where the opening statement was, 'OK. You're on.'
- If you've lost your job because of a company merger or through redundancy, you should prepare a positive explanation concerning what happened. If you've taken a couple of years off to go back to higher education, you ought to speak of the way that experience will benefit you in future jobs.
- For artists, writers, and advertising and public relations executives, showing samples of work can be important at a job interview. If this applies to you, consider what samples you'll want to include and how you will package them.
- Go through your wardrobe and choose two outfits you can wear for interviews (or shop for them, if necessary). That way one will be ready at all times. The outfits should reflect the salary you aspire to earn, and should suit the style of the industry to which you're applying. Conservative attire is appropriate for an

accounting firm, while a bit more flair is suitable for the advertising trade.

■ Choose outfits that make you feel comfortable. You don't want to be fussing with a stiff collar or a wrap-around skirt that won't stay closed during the interview.

The interview

Be on time. Take a minute to make sure you're still looking tidy before you enter the building.

■ Choose a chair that places you comfortably near the interviewer.

■ Try to assess how much time has been allotted for the interview. If the interviewer seems rushed, don't launch into any long stories.

■ If you're not sure what the interviewer is looking for, try to encourage him or her to speak first. Respond accordingly, emphasising your skills and experience.

■ Stick to the business at hand.

■ Work at keeping good eye contact.

■ Be positive about yourself and your attributes, and be enthusiastic about the job.

■ Ask questions about the company to show that you've done some homework.

■ Ask about their time-frame for recruitment. As you leave, you should have a good idea of how much longer they expect to be interviewing for the position.

After the interview

■ As soon as you get home, make notes regarding the job, points discussed and your impressions of the people and the company. This information should be filed in the 'Follow-up' section of your notebook. On a separate sheet of paper (to be filed in the 'Interview preparations' section), note down any points of the conversation that went badly so you can review them before your next interview and benefit from your mistakes.

- Promptly send any additional material the interviewer may have requested.

- Send a thank-you note straight away, emphasising any points you'd like the interviewer to remember (e.g., your experience at fund-raising, your willingness to re-locate).

- If you do not hear from the company within a reasonable time, choose an appropriate date to follow up, mark it in your diary, and call to see what is happening.

- If you don't get through, don't be disheartened. Keep trying. Sometimes people are genuinely so busy they don't have time to return all their calls. Befriend the secretary/PA, and perhaps he or she will tell you the best times to call.

- If you don't get a definite 'no', keep following up until the job is filled. If you do get a 'no', ask for a referral. If you were a serious contender, the interviewer may well have some good suggestions and be pleased to help out.

It may never be a 'perfect' time to look for a job, but remember, you only need one job for the search to be a success. I've always believed that if you work steadily and persistently, you'll get what you want. Just keep trying!

34

Party Planning

While we all know people who can pull a party together at the last minute and have it be a success, for most of us having a successful party requires foresight, thought, co-ordination and a dash of good luck. To be able to have a gathering that both you and your guests can enjoy is an ideal celebration.

General planning: six to eight weeks in advance

- Set a budget.
- Decide on what type of party you will have – a big drinks party, a sit-down dinner, Sunday lunch, a barbecue.
- Set the day, time and place.
- If you're going to need a caterer, select the one you want to use and make certain the caterer is free on that date.
- Buy invitations. You'll need additional time if ordering them.
- Prepare a guest list (use your household notebook), and include on it guests' phone numbers in case you need to call them. After the invitations have been posted, keep the list and use it to keep track of RSVPs.

To do: three to four weeks in advance

- Arrange for extra help if necessary. Will you need someone to serve drinks? Cook? Waiters and waitresses? Babysitter?
- Arrange for entertainment, such as a pianist or a jazz band.
- If the party will be held in cool weather, or if rain is a possibility, think about what you will do with the guests' coats. You may need to rent or borrow a coat-rack.

■ Consider your other needs. If you need to hire or borrow chairs, serving-dishes, glasses, or anything else, make the necessary arrangements.

■ Think about what you want to wear. If you need to shop for something new, do so at least four weeks in advance to allow time for any alterations. If you've chosen something you already own, make sure it is clean and in good repair.

■ Order flowers. If ordering a floral centrepiece for a sit-down affair, be certain to specify a low one. You don't want the arrangement to block the vision of any of the guests at the dinner table.

■ Address and send invitations.

To shop for: three to four weeks in advance

■ Plan your menu. Whether you're serving dinner for eight or just *hors d'oeuvres*, write down each dish you plan to have. If you're working with a caterer, consult with him or her.

■ If you're doing the party on your own, try to select some dishes you can cook ahead and freeze.

■ Assemble all the recipes for the dishes that need to be prepared.

■ Go through the recipes and make a complete list of all ingredients. Even make note of the items you're 'sure' you have. There's nothing worse than discovering you're out of a necessary basic ingredient the day of the party!

■ Check the list against the items you have on hand.

■ Divide the list into categories for easier grocery shopping, or simply transfer the needed items on to one of the shopping lists described in Chapter 27.

■ Go back through the recipes and separate out those dishes that can be made in advance. Also group the recipes that will need to be made at the last minute. (Although I don't recommend last-minute dishes!)

- Consider your drinks needs, not forgetting mixers, soft drinks, lemons and limes, and ice.

- Ask at the off-licence about how much you should get, based on the number of guests who are coming, and their drinking habits.

- You may also need to shop for decorations, paper plates, napkins and cups, place cards, plastic glasses.

- Make sure you have the following on hand: bottle opener, can opener, corkscrew, coasters, hand soaps, ice, ice bucket, matches for candles, napkins, place mats and tablecloth.

- If shopping will be done by more than one person, decide in advance who will purchase what.

To do: one week in advance

- Call to confirm all orders and arrangements, including any help you have coming (cook, waiter or waitress, babysitter, musician), and tell them to arrive earlier than they are really needed. That way, traffic problems or some type of delay won't cause you to panic. They should still arrive well before the guests do.

- Unless you have a 'smoke-free' house, have plenty of ashtrays on hand.

- Be sure you have enough hangers.

Food preparation: one week in advance

- Prepare and freeze any of the dishes that can be made in advance.

To do: one to two days in advance

- Get out the serving-dishes and table linens.

- Get out the china and glasses, and check to see if they need to be washed.

- Get out the silver and see if it needs polishing.

- Clean your home or apartment.

- Think about your space needs for the event. Should the furniture be arranged differently?
- Be sure you have a good supply of paper towels on hand.
- Unless you're paying your helpers by cheque, arrange to have cash.
- Create a time chart to help guide you on the day of the party. Plan at what time you need to set the table (early), when the oven needs to be turned on, and so on. This type of chart is also helpful for anyone who is going to help you. Create a list of their tasks and the time at which each should be done so that everything will go like clockwork.

Food preparation: one to two days in advance

- Organise the dishes that need to be made on the day of the party, especially those (such as stir-frying) that have to be done just prior to or at the time of the meal. Pre-measure as many ingredients as you can and keep them in small dishes or measuring cups, covered in cling film. Group them by recipe in your refrigerator.

To do: the day of the event

- Set the table as early as possible.
- Clear the kitchen work-tops.
- Run the dishwasher before the guests come so that it is empty and ready for the party dishes.
- Do a last-minute straightening of the house, and wipe down the bathrooms to clean off water spots and fingerprints.
- Put out hand towels.

Food preparation: the day of the event

- Get out any of the utensils and dishes you will need for cooking.
- Use a tray to organise the ingredients needed to prepare dishes that must be made just prior to or during the party.

- Use the kitchen timer as a reminder for various things, such as the time to start preparing a certain dish or to take something out of the refrigerator.

- Cheeses should be removed from the refrigerator one hour before being served so that it will reach room temperature.

- Red wine should also be opened an hour in advance so that it can 'breathe'. White wine should be chilled in advance, and can even be opened and re-corked before refrigerating to save you time once your guests arrive.

- Prepare bread baskets in advance.

- Fill ice bucket.

For the Future

- Keep a record in the back of your household notebook (see Chapter 23), or create an 'Entertaining' category in your filing cabinet, which should include a guest list of those who attended as well as those who were unable to come. Note the date, time, and food served, and keep an itemised list of costs. Make notes regarding things that could have gone better, comments on the food, and ideas for the future. This will be helpful in planning another party.

35

Travel Planning

For some people, travel problems begin the moment a trip is being planned – so many unfamiliar things to do, so many details to take care of. What flights will be best? Where shall we stay? What arrangements must be worked out at home? The questions go on and on.

For others, problems don't arise until it's almost time for them to leave: they didn't get as much office work done as they'd intended; they're worried about leaving the children behind; they're exhausted from burning the midnight oil by packing at the last minute; and there's always the nagging feeling that something has been forgotten.

Here are some suggestions that should improve your frame of mind at departure, make your time away more enjoyable, and better prepare you for a smooth return.

Advance planning

- Use a good travel agent, one whose knowledge about routes and fares can save you both time and money. If you are travelling by plane, make sure your agent knows your seating preference (aisle or window), so that he or she can reserve a seat for you ahead of time.

- Call ahead regarding airline meals if you need low-calorie, low- or no-salt, low-cholesterol, vegetarian, kosher or children's meals. You should let your travel agent know your preferences.

- If you're travelling abroad, get hold of enough local currency before you leave to pay for getting to your hotel, making phone calls, and the like.

- Make a photocopy of your passport and take it with you if you're travelling overseas.

- Write an itinerary of your trip. Include phone numbers and addresses of the places you'll be staying each night as well as airline and flight details. Make four copies. Give one copy to someone at work; another copy to the person looking after your house, and take one with you. Pack another copy in your suitcase, so that if your luggage gets lost, it can be sent to you at any stage of your trip.

- At the office, delegate as much as possible. Leave clear instructions as to how certain issues should be handled so that you won't have to do it when you return.

- Look through your diary. Re-schedule any appointments that fall during the time you'll be away.

- Plan for a free day when you return. If you're going on a trip of any length, try to schedule it so that you can stay at home on your first day back. This will give you the time to take care of the washing and cleaning, to pick up the dog, etc.

- Arrange for a friend or neighbour to bring in your post and newspapers so that they don't accumulate. Does someone need to take care of your plants or pet? Leave him or her written instructions as to what to do. You can streamline this process by writing the instructions once. Then make photocopies of the information and file it for future trips. That way you'll never need to write those instructions again.

- If you employ household help, tell them you'll be away and discuss any special tasks to be undertaken. If there is no ironing because you are gone, perhaps you would like to have the cupboards cleaned instead.

- If no one will be at home while you're gone, go through the refrigerator to throw out food that will spoil. Stock up on items you can freeze and use after your return.

- Pack (see Chapter 36). Start this two days prior to departure.

- Confirm your plane reservation and double-check your overnight arrangements.

- Make sure you have some form of photo identification with you.

- Get a copy of a current pocket flight guide. If your plane is cancelled or you miss a flight, you can work out a new flight plan for yourself.

- Buy a phone card, and carry a good supply of coins or notes for tipping.

- Take any phone numbers or travel directions you may need.

- As a welcome home gift, put fresh linens on the bed for your return.

For the children

If children will be staying behind with a grandparent or child-minder, refer to Chapter 52 for additional advice.

Before you walk out the door

- Check to see that you have keys, directions, money (local and foreign), tickets, passport and an itinerary.

- If you live alone or if other family members will be away too, you'll also want to do the following:

  - run the dishwasher early enough that it will have finished before you depart;
  - shut and lock windows;
  - unplug appliances;
  - adjust thermostat;
  - make sure the oven is off;
  - take out the rubbish;
  - leave on a light and/or radio with a timer;
  - lock all doors.

The trip

- Travel in comfortable clothes. Wear a sweater (in the summer you can wear a light cotton one) in case it's chilly on the train, plane or bus. A pair of travel slippers is handy for long flights.

- If you are travelling from cold to warmer weather, consider wearing layered clothing. Upon reaching your destination, you can remove the outer layers and you'll be all set for the new climate!
- If this is a business trip, take along a special file or envelope to keep track of the information and papers you will be collecting (business cards, reports, fliers, receipts, and so on). If your work is going to generate a lot of paperwork, try to handle as much as possible while you're away.
- Plan to arrive at the airport sufficiently early to check in and check your bags before departure.

At the hotel

- When you are first shown to your hotel room, make a quick check of everything. If you're not satisfied, now is the time to discuss the possibility of a room change.
- Once in a satisfactory room, check for the fire exit. Read the hotel literature regarding escape methods.
- Request a hair dryer, ironing board and iron, if needed. Most hotels now supply these at little or no charge.
- If you'll be in a rush the next morning, place your breakfast order with room service the night before.

Your return

While it always feels good to come home, the part that is often the least pleasant is coping with the accumulation of post and messages that have come in while you were away. Here are some tips to help you manage.

- Both at home and at the office, set aside a couple of hours to sort through post and paperwork. Try to do this as soon as possible after your arrival.
- Set priorities on the items you will handle first.
- Try to return all telephone calls at one sitting.

- At the office, check with colleagues about any events that may have occurred while you were away.
- Check your diary so that you're prepared for upcoming events.

36

Travel Packing

Developing a system that works for you will make packing a simple procedure, and will allow you to leave for any type of trip feeling comfortable and well prepared. Let's begin by checking to make sure you have the right travel equipment and accessories.

- Check your luggage to make sure it is roomy and sturdy enough to accommodate what you plan to take. If you're buying new items, look for lightweight bags. Larger pieces should have wheels built into the bottom to make them easier to transport.

- Invest in a good piece of light hand luggage. Styles with wheels can be quite handy. Whenever possible, you should limit your bags to hand luggage to avoid having to wait while the baggage is sorted after the flight.

- Be sure you have luggage labels for your bags (inside and out). Some airlines insist that all suitcases have external labels, so you'll save yourself time at the airport if your bags are already labelled. (If you have a suitcase that looks like everyone else's, tie a fabric ribbon around the handle for easy identification at the baggage carousel.)

- Visit a shop that sells travellers' aids such as small alarm clocks, shower caps, portable washing lines, collapsible plastic hangers, sewing kits, travel irons, electric voltage adapters, and small plastic bottles. But don't buy anything you won't really use.

Planning

Planning is the next step, and several weeks before (when possible) is not too early to begin thinking about what you'll need for the trip. You may need extra time to get shoes repaired or to shop for items you don't already have.

As soon as you know you are going away, begin to prepare a checklist of everything you think you'll need for your trip. Use the checklist below as a starting point.

TRAVEL CHECKLIST

Clothing

_____ Belts	_____ Jeans	Stockings/
_____ Blouses	Pyjamas/	_____ tights
_____ Boots	_____ nightdress	_____ Suits
_____ Coat	_____ Raincoat	_____ Sweaters
_____ Dresses	_____ Scarves	_____ Swimsuit
Dressing	_____ Shirts	_____ Ties
_____ gown	_____ Shoes	_____ Trousers
_____ Gloves	_____ Skirts	_____ Underwear
_____ Hats	_____ Slippers	
_____ Jackets	_____ Socks	

Grooming Items

_____ Aftershave	_____ Mouthwash
_____ Brush, comb	_____ Perfume
_____ Cotton buds	_____ Razor and blades,
_____ Cotton wool	or electric shaver
_____ Creams, lotions	_____ Shampoo,
_____ Dental floss	conditioner
_____ Deodorant	_____ Shaving kit
_____ Feminine needs	_____ Showercap
_____ Hairclips, slides	_____ Soap
_____ Hair curlers,	_____ Sunblock lotion
curling iron	_____ Talc
_____ Hair dryer	_____ Toothbrush
_____ Hair spray	_____ Toothpaste
_____ Make-up	_____ Tweezers
_____ Manicure items	_____ Wet wipes

Medical Items

_____	Adhesive bandages	_____	Insect repellent
_____	Back-up pair of glasses or prescription	_____	Prescription and non-prescription medications
_____	Contact lenses and cleaning solution	_____	Thermometer
_____	First-aid antiseptic ointment	_____	Vitamins

Additional Items

_____	Adaptor (for foreign travel)	_____	Playing cards
_____	Address book	_____	Radio
_____	Alarm clock	_____	Reading material
_____	Camera and film	_____	Safety pins
_____	Cash, traveller's cheques	_____	Scissors
_____	Chequebook	_____	Sewing kit
_____	Credit cards	_____	Stamps
_____	Cufflinks	_____	Sunglasses
_____	Jewellery	_____	Torch
_____	Pen	_____	Travel tickets
		_____	Umbrella
		_____	Contact lenses

- Using the checklist, consider every aspect of your trip and note down clothing, accessories, medications, reading material and emergency supplies. Try to anticipate everything you might need for the locale you'll be in and the kinds of things you'll be doing.

- When planning what clothes to take, prepare for all weather possibilities. When Indian summer turns to crisp autumn overnight, you could be left shivering if you didn't pack a sweater or cardigan of some kind. But be realistic. Overdoing 'just-in-case' items can weigh you down. One person I know took snow hats on a trip to Acapulco just in case the plane had to make an emergency landing in the middle of a snowstorm *en route*. That's what I mean by overdoing it!

- If you're hesitant to leave one or two 'just-in-case' items behind, try to determine whether or not you could purchase the item at your destination if you needed to. A friend felt it was worth travelling with a one-week supply of disposable nappies for her one-year-old when she found out that they were not yet available for purchase where she was visiting overseas. To help you make such decisions, talk to people who have recently visited the places you are going.

- Avoid excess bulk. Select clothes that co-ordinate, and keep your choices to a minimum. Most of us take too much.

- Buy a small folding clothes rail where you can display all items of clothing before you pack them. Seeing your clothes together often helps you eliminate the excess or discover a problem (missing button, stain on shirt, etc.). Many clients have reported night-before-departure panic when they realise that a favourite suit needed cleaning and there was no time to get it done. It's important to pack your clothes in first-class condition – clean, unwrinkled, and ready to wear.

The 'ever-ready' toiletry kit

When it comes to packing, a permanently prepared toiletry kit is a must. Why pack and re-pack the same items every trip?

- For the kit, choose a small case (preferably a transparent, soft-sided, waterproof bag). The number of toiletries to be packed should be the determining factor as to bag size.

- Invest in an extra toothbrush, razor and hairbrush to keep permanently packed in your travel kit.

- Buy travel-sized toothpaste, shampoo and aspirin, reserved for travel use.

- Transfer items such as your facial cleanser into small plastic bottles (available at travel shops and chemists). Any liquids you must take should be in tightly sealed plastic containers, only three-quarters full, and put in secured plastic bags. At the end of each trip, refill any containers that are getting low.

- Compartmentalise your toiletry bag for easy retrieval. Divide essentials into categories: body care (lotion, deodorant), make-up (foundation, lipstick), hair care (shampoo, conditioner), and dental items (toothpaste, toothbrush, and floss).

- Try to travel with as few spillables as possible. Any you must take should be wrapped and packed very carefully, preferably in your toiletry bag. To reduce the risk, carry doubtful items on the plane with you.

- Use scented body or hand lotion instead of perfume. It saves space and avoids the chance of costly spills.

- Call ahead regarding hair dryers. Many hotels now provide them, and this will mean you'll have one less thing to bring.

Your hand luggage

For trips during which you'll check in some of your luggage, you'll still want good hand luggage. Items that are too important to be without and that will make plane travel more pleasant are those you'll pack in your hand luggage.

- Buy a lightweight, compartmentalised bag (smaller than the carry-on bag you would use for clothes for a short trip).

- Plan to carry tickets, jewellery, essential toiletries, important papers, a pocket flight guide, maps, money, your address book, and passport.

- To pass the time, have on hand your laptop, business material you haven't had time to study, a novel you've been longing to read, or personal stationery with which to catch up on correspondence.

- The air inside the cabin on a plan can be very dry, so, for additional comfort, take a small tube of moisturiser or hand lotion to keep you feeling refreshed. Men might carry a disposable razor for a quick shave before reaching their destination. Other items to consider carrying on board might

include moist towellettes, toothbrush and toothpaste, tissues, a
small container of freshening facial cleanser, and a pen and
pocket-sized notebook for jotting down thoughts, questions, and
ideas.

Packing

You should actually begin putting items in your bags about two days
before your departure. It's too tiring to pack the night before when
you'll have other details to take care of such as last-minute instructions
to colleagues or to the person who will be watching the house, and so
forth. (I shudder when I think of one friend who is always up until
3 a.m. the night before her trip doing laundry and ironing.)

- Begin by hanging or laying out your garments.
- When departing with more than one piece of luggage, divide
  your clothes among the suitcases. This avoids being left with
  only a suitcase full of your shoes and underwear while your bag
  filled with suits and dresses is lost.
- To transport your clothes wrinkle-free, save any tissue paper
  acquired in presents and purchases to fold with your clothing
  when packing. Some people like to roll their clothing rather than
  laying it flat. With some items it takes up less room and can
  prevent wrinkling.
- Put heavier, most wrinkle-resistant items (sweaters and jeans) on
  the bottom. To minimise wasted space, alternate the layers of
  remaining clothes: first, a layer from left to right, then one from
  front to back.
- Store underwear and hosiery in separate, transparent plastic bags,
  and tuck them into the corners of your suitcase.
- Pack items inside one another. For example, socks and shoehorn
  should go inside shoes, hosiery inside a folded sweater.
- Put your shoes, paired, in plastic bags or cloth shoe-bags and
  place them along the sides of the suitcase as you are packing.
  Since these will probably be the heaviest items in your luggage,
  keep them to a minimum.

- The nooks and crannies that remain should be filled with rolled-up belts, socks and scarves. These items will cushion and hold the other items when the suitcase is closed and standing upright.

- If you can anticipate your needs ahead of time, make sure that the last layer of clothing you pack will be the articles you will need first upon your arrival.

- Plastic bags are useful for laundry and to hold clothes that may be damp.

- Some people like to pack clothes on their hangers. Women may want to take along extra skirt hangers.

- Add a potpourri sachet to keep your clothes smelling fresh.

- When packing to come home, you may fear you'll never be able to fit in the extras you bought. Roll your clothing instead of laying it flat.

- Keep your checklist! While there will always be variations in clothing, it will serve as a helpful guide in packing the next time. You need never forget your address book or sunglasses again!

Personal Agenda

37

Beauty Routine

once needed to attend a meeting with a beauty/fashion consultant and since we lived quite close to each other, we decided to share a taxi into the centre of town. I was very surprised when she came downstairs and got into the taxi with no make-up on. She then proceeded to pull out a small bag and spent 10 of the 15 minutes we were in the taxi applying foundation, eye make-up, blusher and lipstick. When we arrived, she looked terrific!

Since most of us can't count on having a hands-free taxi ride for doing our make-up (let alone having the ability to apply make-up while bumping up and down), it's important to establish a simple beauty regime that becomes an easy and natural part of the day.

The key to an efficient beauty routine lies partly in organising your supplies so they are accessible and convenient, but it also has to do with making the routine a matter of habit.

Here's how to get started.

Simplifying your morning routine

- Consider your haircut. With today's easy styles, there is no reason to have one that requires much effort. Choose a cut that is easy to care for, and then get it trimmed regularly so that you benefit fully from the easy styling.

- Consider your skin care system. Are you mixing and matching various soaps and moisturisers depending on what's handy that day? Instead, choose one basic skin care treatment, perhaps one where all the products are designed to go together. It will be easier to follow, and you'll have two or three products to store instead of more.

- Consider your make-up routine. Try to establish one or two simple 'looks', using a minimal number of products. Visit a make-up consultant at one of your local department stores to help you select complementary products and make a fresh start.

Organising your make-up

- Evaluate the area where you put on your make-up. Is this the best place to do it? Is the lighting good? Is there a convenient spot for storing your make-up? If you apply your make-up in the bathroom, select a convenient place to store it.

- Go through your make-up and throw out what you no longer use. Also throw out those items that are more than a year old or that you think you might not use again – you probably won't, and make-up doesn't age well, anyway. Some products gather bacteria and can even be dangerous to use if allowed to sit for a long period of time.

- Buy a compartmentalised plastic caddy for your make-up with separate slots for lipstick and brushes, and places for foundation and blusher.

- Within the caddy, organise the items by type. For example, store all brushes in one spot, all lipsticks in another, and all eye shadows in another. Items used first (or most frequently) should be most accessible.

- Consider an all-purpose make-up kit (available at most department stores), complete with co-ordinated eye, cheek and lip colours.

- When your make-up needs to be altered with the changing of the seasons (more moisturising products for winter; lighter products for summer), pack away the cosmetics you don't use during the current season.

- When you find a product that works, stick with it.

- Keep lotion and hand cream in all the rooms where you use it – in the bathroom, the kitchen and the bedroom. A pump-style lotion dispenser saves times, and for double duty, rub cream or lotion into your cuticles while you're applying it to your hands.

- Use clear nail polish. It's easier to touch up if it gets chipped, and it doesn't need to be applied as frequently as coloured polish.

- Pick up travel-sized make-up items and extras of lipstick, mascara and blusher to store in a make-up bag at the office or to carry with you in your handbag.

- For travel, keep a lightweight make-up bag stocked and ready to go with all your essentials. Stock up on travel-sized quantities of skin care and make-up items, and buy sample sizes of items such as lotion and shampoo. When you get home, replace your travel supplies so you'll automatically be ready for the next trip.

Establishing your routine

Next time you take a trip, note how much more you must concentrate on applying your make-up simply because your products aren't where your hands are trained to find them. If you've not yet developed a system that your hands seem to perform automatically, you haven't simplified your routine as much as possible. Here's how to do so.

- Choose a specific time of day (after your morning shower or before breakfast) when you apply your make-up, and do it at that same time every day, including weekends. The more automatically the routine is performed, the more quickly you can do it.

- Establish a set routine for putting on your make-up (concealer followed by foundation, followed by powder, etc.).

- In the morning, stay in one room until you've finished everything you need to do there. For example, after your shower, stay in the bathroom and do your make-up while you're waiting for your hair to dry.

- Establish a set time for appointments such as monthly manicures so they become an expected part of your schedule.

- 'Double up' on time. Time spent commuting can be perfect for muscle-firming exercises. If you're not driving, you can also touch up your make-up. Time spent watching the news or your favourite television programme is a perfect opportunity to give yourself a manicure. And before sitting down at your desk, give yourself a facial that can work while you pay your bills.

38

Dates to Remember

My husband is often late with cards and presents. After he'd forgotten to buy anything for our ninth wedding anniversary, I put him on 'notice' and said he had one year to plan for our tenth. So there would be no excuses, I kept reminding him as the date grew nearer. On the morning of our anniversary, he did present me with a wonderful present – but much to his chagrin, he'd still forgotten the card!

If you've cornered the market on belated birthday cards (or even if you've only missed one or two special dates this year), you're causing yourself needless frustration by having forgotten to send good wishes to someone you care about.

When it comes to special occasions, late is better than never, but nothing beats being on time. All that's required for remembering important dates is a simple system that works for you. Here are several from which to choose.

The birthday book

Stationery, gift and speciality shops usually sell special date-books (or 'birthday books') that are designed for keeping track of special occasions. Museum gift shops frequently have ones that are especially beautiful. One advantage of the birthday book is that it can be used year after year, so you need to record only once the dates you want to remember.

- Buy a birthday book you find appealing. (You may want to buy two or three – they make great gifts!)
- Enter all the special occasions of which you want to be reminded.

- As you make each entry, also note the year of birth or, for anniversaries, the year of the marriage. That way you can always figure out how old Mary's son is, and 40th birthdays and silver wedding anniversaries won't slip by without appropriate celebration.

- Consult your birthday book at the end of each month to note the special dates for the weeks ahead.

- The only way the birthday book can fail you is if you forget to use it. If you're just starting out with this system, make a note in your calendar or tickler file (see below) for the next few months to remind yourself to consult your book.

Diary reminders

If you don't think you can adjust to referring to a special book regularly, a diary reminder method whereby you note a person's birthday or a special occasion on the upcoming year's diary may work better for you. (If you're working with a diary on computer or one of the hand-held electronic organisers, this information will transfer from year to year, saving you the time of re-writing it.)

- Go through your diary today and note all special occasions you intend to remember.

- Use a special colour of ink, perhaps red or turquoise, to distinguish these notes from other information.

- In late December, sit down and transfer all the dates from the old diary to the new one. Because you've used a special colour, the entries should pop out at you, thus minimising the chance of error when making the annual date transfer.

Tickler files

Your tickler files (see Chapter 11) offer another simple way to be reminded of special occasions. With this system, you'll pull out your reminder at the beginning of each month.

- Using a separate card for each month, record special occasions on index cards, which can then be filed in the appropriate file folders.

- In order to plan and buy in advance, put the February card in the January file (so that in January you'll be thinking of the February dates you need to shop for), and the March card in the February file, and so on. This gives you enough warning to plan for occasions falling early in the following month.

Following through

Regardless of the system you choose, nothing works unless you follow through.

- Establish a regular time each month to review upcoming dates and shop for all the cards or presents you will need in the coming weeks.

- Purchase a selection of blank cards that will serve a variety of purposes (get well, congratulations, thank you, happy birthday) for those times when something unexpected comes up.

- When you arrive home with your newly purchased cards, address and sign each one. Write the date they need to be posted in the corner where the stamp should go. Store the cards in a mail or 'out' basket near your front door and put a stamp on them the day they are to be sent. (Keep a small supply of stamps in the out basket.)

By choosing and using one of these systems, you can say goodbye to those last-minute dashes to the shops to get a card or present. (For tips on shopping for presents for special occasions, see Chapter 40.)

39
Errands

How many times have you arrived home from doing errands, only to remember that there was something you forgot? As you venture back out, it may seem like the errands are running you rather than the other way around!

The main difficulty people encounter with running errands is they forget to plan ahead. One day I dropped in on my neighbour to see if she needed any help with arrangements for a party she was having that night. She said how tired she was from going to the shops. Well, it turned out she wasn't tired from one trip to the shops; she was tired from three. Each time she had come back home, she remembered something else she needed and had to go back out again!

With a little creative planning, you can avoid these last-minute dashes and streamline the chores that otherwise fill your free time.

Establishing a system

- An ongoing list is the first step in getting errands done more efficiently. I recommend using your loose-leaf household notebook (see Chapter 23). Establish a section for items 'To buy' (light-bulbs, gloves), 'To fix' (the suit that needs to go to the tailor, or the doll that needs to be taken in for repair), and 'To do' (donate blood, drop in at the library, check new hotel as a possible place for Mum and Dad to stay). Then you can transfer the items you plan to do each day on to your 'To do' list in your calendar. Or if you plan a full day of errands, simply take the notebook with you.

- Teach family members to tell you about general errands (shoes that need re-heeling, shirts for the laundry, a toaster that needs mending, etc.) that must be entered into your notebook. Also make it clear that family members should let you know when the supply of items to be purchased (such as shaving cream, shampoo, transparent tape, index cards) is low, not out.

- Anticipate upcoming needs. Buy a season's supply of tights or stockings, several booklets of stamps, and five or six tubes of toothpaste (especially if you catch a sale!) at the same time.

- Establish a table, desk or chair near the front door where you can lay out all you need for upcoming errands (suits for the cleaners; an item to be returned to the shop). Your keys, wallet or purse, and briefcase should also be located here for an easy exit.

Consolidating your errands

- Always plan your errands around your schedule, not the other way around.

- On Sunday evening, sit down with your household notebook and your diary, which should also have space for each day's 'To do' list. Are any of your upcoming appointments in an area of town where you can accomplish another chore? If so, write a reminder in your diary for that day.

- For regular errands to be done during the week, select one or two blocks of time (after work on Tuesday; during lunch-time on Thursday), when you can conveniently get some errands done. Then list on your diary what you plan to accomplish.

- Organise your errands by location. For example, before going out to do errands around your local area, work out a route so that each stop takes you part of the way to the next one. Once you've finished, you can go directly on to your next activity or plan a circular route that brings you back home again.

- Try to shop during periods of least activity – mid-morning rather than noon, for example.

Carry-all convenience

- Buy an unstructured nylon bag to use for errands. These are light, completely collapsible (keep it in your briefcase or car, just

in case), and easy to wipe out in case of spills. Many feature a
long strap for shoulder-carrying.

- Also buy a waterproof that folds into a small pouch. They are
  lighter and more compact than a telescopic umbrella when not
  in use, and when you are using them, your hands are kept free.
  Also have an extra plastic shopping bag or two to cover or to
  carry packages in the rain.

On the go

It's your turn to pay at the checkout, you're balancing several parcels,
the man behind you is in a rush, and you can't find the right credit card
. . . Sound familiar? A few tips may help out.

- In your wallet, categorise your money by denomination. Don't
  run the risk of giving someone a £20 note when you meant to
  give him £10.
- Alphabetise your credit cards so you'll quickly be able to find the
  one you want.
- Organise your handbag for convenient shopping (see Chapter
  41). Items you may need on your errands – shopping list, pen,
  calculator – should be kept in an outer flap or some other easily
  accessible spot.
- Since you will need your shopping receipts when you get home,
  always ask for the receipts to be handed to you rather than
  dropped in the bag. Then store them in one part of your wallet,
  handbag or briefcase where you can sort through them later.
- Always carry some change for a phone call, and a phone card.

Coming home

'What do you do when you get home with all the packages?' asked one
of my clients who told a story about how she had been putting things
away for half an hour one night when she realised she hadn't even taken
off her coat.

Other people tend to arrive home, dump their packages, and let days
go by before putting everything away.

Remember the chair or table near the door? Well, that's your home base for arrival too. Here's how to proceed from there.

■ Unload all parcels as you come in.

■ As soon as you've put away your coat and hat, return and start putting things away.

■ Begin by putting away perishables.

■ Categorise items by room to avoid unnecessary trips.

■ Unwrap items as you go and cut off labels and plastic tags before putting them away. You may be in a rush the first day you need them.

Tips to save wear and tear

■ Take advantage of any local shop who will pick up and deliver.

■ Any time you can find a professional – manicurist, hairdresser, exercise instructor – who will come to your home or office, take advantage of it.

■ If you have extra time before or after an appointment, pull out your notebook and see what you can get done.

■ If you happen to pass by a speciality shop and remember something you need, go in and buy it right away.

■ Prepare for possible waiting time during the errand-running process. Write down a menu, plan a party list in your notebook, or read while you're waiting in a queue.

■ Ask family members to help out with errands.

What to do when you dread doing an errand

We all have certain things we just hate doing, like returning an item or dropping something off at the dry cleaners which is right on the other side of town. Here's how to overcome your own resistance.

■ Ask, 'What will happen if I don't do this task?' If there are no dire consequences, forget it.

- Co-operate. Team up with another parent for buying supplies for a school picnic, for example.
- Swap. If your neighbour will shop for something you need near his office, offer to do something special for him.
- Nervous about returning merchandise? Enlist a friend for moral support.
- Pay someone to do it for you. It might be worth it!

40

Shopping for Presents

How often have you received one of the following as a present:

- A shirt or blouse two sizes too big or too small?
- A sweater in a colour you detest and would never wear?
- An outfit that would have been perfect for you five years ago?
- An absolutely useless knick-knack?

While there is no way to prevent others from giving you the unwanted and the unusable, you can avoid contributing to the white elephant collection of others by organising your present-buying system.

By making present-buying a year-round process you will save time (no rushing around at the last minute) and money (how often have you said, 'I don't care what it costs, I need a present for tonight!'). You'll also find that your presents are more appreciated because they'll show the thought and planning that went into them.

Buying presents for others is a two-step process. First, you need to remember that a birthday or anniversary is drawing near (see Chapter 38); then you need to have a system for choosing an appropriate present.

Establishing a system

- Establish a Presents file in your filing cabinet (as suggested in Chapter 11) where you can store present lists as well as cuttings and articles about perfect presents for family and friends.
- Buy index cards.
- On the front of each card, write the name of a friend, family member or business associate with whom you exchange presents. (This could also be done on your computer, but make a printout for your file.) Note the date of birth, and other important

occasions. Make notes about the person's likes and dislikes. Note sizes, favourite colours, hobbies and special interests. The front of the card will also be used for noting present ideas. Whenever you think of a terrific present idea, write it down immediately! The front of a card for a friend might look like this:

TRACY ROLANDS

Birthday: 11 March, 1960   Blouse size: 12

Favourite colours: pink and blue   Sweater: medium

Collects antique clothing and loves floppy hats
Hobbies include photography and home restoration
Present ideas: handmade photo albums (at craft market); also try
antiques auction for other ideas

- On the back of the card, keep a running record of what you give each year. That way you'll avoid giving the same present twice. A sample card for your father might look like this:

DAD

Birthday 1996   book on coin-collecting
Christmas 1996   shirt and tie
Birthday 1997   engraved shoe horn
Christmas 1997   V-neck sweater

- How to use the system? At the beginning of each month, when you consult your birthday book (see Chapter 38) or tickler file and note down whose birthday is coming up, simply go to your Presents file and pull out the appropriate index cards. You've automatically got all the information you need to buy a thoughtful, personal present!

Getting it done

- See Chapter 39 for tips on faster, easier shopping.

- Scout around small boutiques and speciality shops where you can shop for unusual items without having to fight long queues. When you do need to shop in department stores, go as soon as the stores open, when they're likely to be less crowded.

- 'Buy it when you see it' is a good rule of thumb. Make all types of present-buying (even Christmas) a year-round project. If you wait, you may have difficulty finding the item that seemed so perfect when you saw it a few months ago.

- Shopping by mail order is a time-saver. That item you saw while flipping through a catalogue may solve the dilemma of what to give your dad for Father's Day.

- When you get home, wrap it up! Almost as bad as not having a present on hand is discovering at the last minute that the one you have isn't wrapped. Note its contents on a detachable label. Or if you know who will receive it, put on the appropriate gift tag.

- Keep extra presents on hand for unexpected needs. Stock up on exotic mustards, spices, jams and vinegars, which can be attractively packed in a basket or box for a handy last-minute present.

- Consider presents that don't require shopping: a magazine subscription (roll up a current issue and put a bow around it); tickets to the theatre, a concert, or sports event; membership in a local museum; a handwritten card informing the person of something you've set up for them – a massage, a class, a visit to a palm reader or psychic; an IOU offering to clean a cupboard or babysit.

If you implement these suggestions, what happened to my cousin won't happen to you. At the last minute, she realised that she hadn't purchased a present for her friend's birthday. Then she remembered an unopened bottle of fine wine she had received as a present a few months before. How embarrassed she was when the present was opened and her friend pointed out that it was the same present she had given my cousin for her last birthday!

41

Handbag

When I give a speech about getting organised to a group of women, I often begin my talk by requesting that they take out their handbags and see how quickly they can locate 10p for a telephone call. You'd be surprised how few women can produce one! What would happen if I put that test to you?

You should have an organised handbag. It's a nuisance to have to take several moments to fish for a pen, and it's nothing short of dangerous not to be able to put your hands on your car or house keys quickly at night.

First, you'll need a well-made, functional bag. Choose one with pockets and zipped compartments for categorising your belongings. Avoid a shapeless bag; the contents will scatter everywhere within it and you'll constantly be hunting for what you need.

You may want to select a nylon or vinyl bag for wet weather. The contents will stay dry and it can be wiped off easily once you're at home or in the office.

What to carry? Keep it simple. Here are the necessities and some tips for each.

- Wallet or purse. Categorise your money by denomination, small notes first. If you have a purse with two sections for change, put coins in one side and 10p and 20p pieces for telephone calls in the other.

- Credit card holder. Alphabetise your cards within the holder. Don't forget to make a list of cards and their numbers. Keep one copy of the list at home and one at work, in case you should ever have to cancel them in a hurry.

You can double up on the above by shopping for a wallet or purse which has a big enough section for credit cards. It's easier to manage; however, you do run the risk of losing everything if it's stolen.

- Keys. Keep them in a pocket or compartment within your bag so they are easily accessible. Identify them by number or use different colours of nail polish to code them, but don't put your name and address on the key-ring.

- Day planner. Use only one appointment diary, and carry this with you at all times (see Chapter 8).

- Small telephone directory. Carry frequently called telephone numbers here.

- Business card case. Keep the case in a special part of your handbag or briefcase where it can be easily located. At meetings, slip it in your pocket for greater convenience.

- Pen and paper (or small spiral notebook). Handy for jotting down notes and things to do.

- Reading material. Always have something with you in case you encounter an unexpected delay.

- Small zip-up bag. This can serve one of three purposes:
  - use it as a bag within a bag. At lunch, transfer valuables, money, keys, and your calendar to the small bag and leave your big bag at the office;
  - keep all of your cosmetics here;
  - use it to hold receipts, business cards, and other items given to you during the day.

Take along for the unexpected

- On-the-go survival kit. In your cosmetics bag or in another small pouch, pack a safety pin or two, plasters, packaged moist towellettes, lip balm, tissues, aspirin, and needle and thread.

- Stockings or tights. An extra pair comes in handy when the ones you're wearing run on the way to an important function. Roll them into a small ball and store in a small plastic bag to keep from snagging in your handbag.

- Paper towels. On a day when rain is predicted, slip in a few extra paper towels or a hand towel to help dry off your face and hands if you get soaked. (If you're wearing boots that day, carry your shoes in a plastic bag with a drawstring, available at some shoe stores.)

Make a habit of sorting through your wallet or purse daily. Take out notes, receipts, and information gathered while out; process them; and make sure your are re-supplied for the next day.

42

Briefcase

When you travel the streets of a big city, where people walk or take public transport, you begin to realise that men and women use their briefcase to carry everything: I've seen people carrying their lunch, their laundry, and even their pet. Some people pack their case so full that they lean to one side as they carry it.

The most important thing to remember about a briefcase is that its primary purpose is to transport items (usually papers) from one place to another. It is not a suitcase; it is not a store-room; it is not a place to pack everything you were afraid to leave behind. It is your briefcase. Pack it carefully and it will serve you well.

Shopping for a Briefcase

- Basically, briefcases come in two styles: a hard-sided suitcase type and an expandable type. Personal preference (or the style carried by people in your industry) should dictate which style you choose. However, remember that the expandable type tends to be lighter, though it doesn't always preserve papers as well as the hard-sided style since there's a tendency to overstuff it.

- Look for a briefcase that totally seals so that papers don't get wet in rain or snow.

- A good briefcase has pockets and at least one zippered inside compartment where you can put your belongings. Some briefcases have sections specifically designed to hold items such as pens, calculators, notebook-size computers, and the like.

- If a style you like doesn't have inner pockets or compartments, you can buy a small zipped travel bag or transparent pencil case to serve this purpose.

- Many people like a pocket on the outside where they can slip their newspaper or magazine for reading in transit.
- Expandable briefcases sometimes come with removable shoulder straps. This can be a real plus for hands-free carrying. If that style doesn't work well for you for everyday use, consider looking for an inexpensive one with a shoulder strap for air travel. Being able to put the briefcase on your shoulder makes it easier to handle your hand baggage.
- Many women find that having a briefcase that doubles as a handbag is an additional convenience.

What to carry

Here are some suggested items to carry. For convenience, they are broken down into categories.

- Must Have:
  - business cards;
  - pad of paper;
  - pen or pencil with eraser;
  - reading material;
  - diary and address book, or electronic organiser/palmtop computer (to have with you at all times)

- Would Like to Have:
  - calculator;
  - envelopes;
  - extra file folders;
  - highlighter;
  - paper clips;
  - stamps;
  - Post-it notes.

- Might come in Handy:
  - extra set of keys;

- moist towellettes;
- nail file and clipper;
- pain relievers and plasters;
- small tape recorder, or dictaphone;
- small sewing kit, such as the ones provided by some hotels;
- stockings or tights (roll and store in a small plastic bag).

■ All small items (pen, stamps, aspirin, sewing kit) should be kept in the compartments of your briefcase (or in small travel bags) for accessibility. Keep personal items in one compartment, desk supplies in another.

■ Make sure that all papers you carry are put in their own folder and labelled appropriately. (Some people prefer to use manila envelopes.) Within the briefcase, folders can be in chronological order according to the stops you'll be making, or in alphabetical order.

Other tips

■ If you have a business meeting, make a list of what you'll need. Pack your briefcase according to the list. If your list is handy, you'll have an easy way to do a last-minute cross-check to see that you're ready for the meeting.

■ Your briefcase should be thoroughly re-organised at least once a week. Re-supply as needed and be certain that items such as your calculator are in good working order. Don't forget to clean out old papers.

43
How to Stop Losing Things

Although most people have at some time left an umbrella in a taxi, misplaced a favourite pen, or dropped a glove somewhere, far more often we are frustrated at losing something because we know it's right there in front of us – if only we could find it!

One client was fairly efficient about most things, but he didn't have a system for items he used occasionally. Every trip to the library was preceded by an annoying search of the house for the place where he had last put his library card.

Another person I know simply had no system for anything. She was constantly losing things, but the magnitude of her problem didn't really strike me until the time she bought something and lost it on the way home from the shop!

The old saying 'A place for everything and everything in its place' takes the misery out of losing things. Here are some simple ways to make it work for you.

Don't scatter – categorise

- Items used frequently should be placed within easy reach.
- Infrequently used items should be stored away so they don't clutter up the storage areas for more frequently needed things.
- Items that are alike should be kept together. (All stamps, paper, envelopes, and pens or pencils should be stored in or near your desk; hair-clips, slides and combs should have a special box or drawer in your bedroom.)
- Items used together should be stored together. For example, establish a bag where you keep all items for a trip to the beach.

- Items should be stored near where they are used. (Exercise equipment should be kept in the room where you use it; shopping bags should be near the front door.)
- How to make the system work? When you've finished with something, put it back in its place right away.

Establish a permanent home for frequently used one and only items

Here are two examples.

- Keys. A special hook, drawer, or bowl on a shelf near the door is a good place for them. Always put them there!
- Glasses. If you mainly wear them for desk work, keep them in your briefcase or in your desk drawer. If you wear them for driving, keep them in your handbag or near the front door.

Storage tips

- Use colour-coding or written labels on boxes for items stored on deep or high shelves. Label everything!
- Egg cartons, film cartons or even home-made drawer partitions fashioned from cardboard can be a great help in categorising small things. Be imaginative!
- Establish a shelf or box for giveaway items. Add to it as you find things you're tempted to throw away.
- Designate a drawer or shelf as a place for presents you purchase ahead of time.

44

Organising Your Partner

When it comes to 'organising' your partner, tolerance will have to be the order of the day. You won't survive as a couple if one tries totally to reform the other. Helpful resolves are the following.

- I respect his or her right to live the way he or she is most comfortable.
- I reserve the right to request certain changes so that his or her sloppiness or disorganisation no longer affects me or impedes the overall functioning of the household.

For example, I am more efficient than my husband at getting ready for things, so when we travel, I'm responsible for all the packing. He's responsible for bringing the keys and loading and unloading the car. Rather than argue that I am doing most of the work, I simply accept what he can do in this situation. Then in other parts of our life, such as with our tax returns, he does the lion's share of the work.

So after you've tried yelling, pleading, and other desperate tactics, think 'compromise', and improve what you can by using the following tips.

Establishing a system

- Co-ordinate schedules. Establish at least two nights (such as Wednesday and Sunday) when you sit down together and compare diaries. Make sure that each of you records the plans that affect you both.
- Provide him or her with a specific space so that his or her habits have less effect on you. Separate desks, shelves, cupboards and suitcases are a good investment.

- A colour-coding system will help identify towels, toothbrushes and cups.

- When it comes to household chores, ask for his or her input and you'll get more co-operation. A discussion may reveal that he hates to vacuum but doesn't mind washing the dishes. If you don't mind vacuuming, you can each do what you feel is a tolerable chore and thus avoid an argument.

- Divide tasks fairly. Each of you can take certain chores or parts of chores. For example, for a dinner party, let her do the shopping and you do the cooking. A task chart of what must be done each week or day by day will sort out responsibilities.

Hoping for modest reform

- Set a good example. You can't force organisation, but you can encourage it.

- Inspire your partner. If your desk is constantly clear, he or she may be interested in learning from you.

- Communicate. Show him/her exactly where things belong. How do you want the health records filed so that you can find them again? Where do the out-of-season clothes belong? How should the medicine cabinet be arranged?

- Don't become a personal valet. If you always do the picking up, your partner has no reason to do it. It may be as simple as a lesson. Your husband simply may not know how to fold a sweater. Or your wife might not understand the importance of setting up a Personal Property Inventory.

- Give positive reinforcement. It can help!

I remember a sketch which featured a woman obsessed by tidiness. Her husband came home from work and she just couldn't stop cleaning. If he got up from his chair, she would clean the seat; she dusted the floor where he walked; the ashtray he used; and so. One night he couldn't stand it any more, so he took out a gun to shoot her. The end of the scene showed her dusting off the gun and the floor before she fell. So, inspire, but don't seek total reform!

45

Wardrobe Shopping for Women

Have you ever gone on a shopping trip when you walked into a shop and became so confused and overwhelmed you turned around and walked straight out again?

Or have you ever gone shopping, intending to buy one red sweater and walked out with two instead – one green and one blue?

Have you ever come home with a great skirt only to have it hang in your wardrobe, never worn, because you didn't make time to shop for the 'perfect' blouse to go with it?

Everyone has mistakes hanging in their wardrobes – the dress you bought to wear 'when I lose some weight', or the outfit that 'really isn't me after all . . .'

But when the mistakes in the wardrobe outnumber the rest of your clothes, you know you're doing something wrong. It's time to re-think your shopping methods.

With thought and planning, you can build a co-ordinated wardrobe that will give you more outfits, with fewer purchases, than you have now. Here's how.

Planning your new wardrobe

- Consider your budget. This will help you keep your shopping goals in perspective and force you to focus on what you really need. For example, in order to build a good wardrobe for work, you may not be able to add new casual clothes this spring, but those can be the first thing you buy in the autumn.

- Co-ordination is the key to a successful wardrobe. To achieve this, you will need to build your wardrobe around a colour scheme. Begin by choosing two major colours in which you look good. The two colours (for example, black and ivory) should work well together so that the items you buy will easily co-ordinate. That way you'll have twice as many outfits from the same number of pieces.

- Weed through your current wardrobe. Take everything out of your wardrobe, drawers and shelves (see Chapter 24). Discard items you haven't worn in the past two years. (Honestly, if you haven't worn it after several years, you probably never will.) With the other items, ask, 'Is this still fashionable? Do I look good in it?' (Don't guess. Try it on.) 'Do I still like it?'

- Of the remaining items, decide which ones you want to use as a base for your new wardrobe. Select the clothing that makes you look good and feel comfortable. You may have a wonderful jacket and blouse, or one good suit you'd like to use as your base item. Keep your work and lifestyle requirements in mind.

- Make a list of what you need to fill in with your basic wardrobe items and put this list in your household notebook (see Chapter 23) under 'To buy'. The list will give you an action plan for your shopping trip and should help you avoid impulse buying. (Remember, that's how you ended up with most of the mistakes you have now!)

- Organise your list into categories (shoes, accessories, etc.).

- Look through magazines and tear out pictures of fashions you like. Paste these in your notebook as a reminder.

Planning the shopping trip

- Plan to devote the better part of a day to your first shopping trip. A couple of hours just isn't enough time. (But don't shop so long that you get over-tired. It will affect your decision-making.)

- Think ahead about where you'd like to shop. Where are your favourite shops? Plan to restrict each trip to a single geographical area so you can focus on accomplishing the task at hand.

- Of course, you'll need to take a list with you. If you have a portable household notebook, fine. Otherwise, I usually recommend you carry just the appropriate pages with you. Or you can go through the household notebook list and transfer relevant information (what you plan to shop for on this expedition) to your diary 'To do' list, which you should have with you at all times.

Getting ready

- Wear an outfit that will simplify trying clothes on in the shops. If you're shopping for a new item to co-ordinate with something you already have, try to wear it rather than carry it.

- If you're choosing a skirt to go with a blouse and jacket you already have and you decide not to wear them, you'll need to take the blouse and jacket with you. It can be difficult to remember the lines of clothing well enough to know if the 'look' will be right once you have on all three pieces.

- Avoid wearing anything that has lots of buttons; don't wear a turtleneck pullover that can be hard to pull on over your head, high boots, or lots of jewellery, which can get tangled.

- Wear a hairstyle that keeps the hair out of your face but can be neatened easily once you've finished in the fitting room.

- Wear (or take) the bra you'll be wearing with the outfit for which you're shopping. If you're trying on evening wear, be sure to take the appropriate lingerie.

- Choose comfortable shoes that are easy to slip on and off.

- If you will be having a dress or skirt hem adjusted, take (or wear) the shoes you intend to wear with the outfit. (If you need just a rough idea of how the heel height will affect the dress, carry along only one of the shoes.)

- Take a lightweight shoulder bag. A big bag tends to get in the way when you're combing through racks and carrying clothing into the dressing room. A heavy one also makes you tire faster simply because you're carrying the added weight.

When shopping

- Think co-ordination. Aim to create a variety of outfits from three or four pieces.

- Go for the classics. If you want to be stylish, try to adapt a classic outfit to the fashions of the season. Or add this year's accessories to a more conservative outfit you already own. Steer clear of hard-to-wear accessories, however. If you're not comfortable when you try it on, it won't improve with time.

- Try on everything! Just because a sweater is marked medium doesn't mean it will fit you properly. I know several women who buy without trying on, but if I dared to do that, I'd spend the rest of my life returning clothes to the shops.

- If you find a pair of trousers, shoes, or a blouse you look great in, consider buying two. If it's perfect for you and you can use more than one colour of the same style, it's a good investment.

- Judge each article of clothing based on how you feel in it. Even if it's a beautiful outfit, you've got to feel good about yourself.

- Check the garment care label. Is the item going to be more trouble than it's worth?

- Avoid impulse purchases. Stick to your list.

- Don't buy what you don't need or won't wear again.

Other tips

- Consider using a personal shopper. With working women having less and less time to shop, these services are becoming available in more and more department stores. Sometimes a small fee is charged. A personal shopper accompanies you throughout the store, then all garments are taken back to one fitting room for a trying-on session. Sometimes your shopper will even pull out some appropriate outfits in advance. If sizes are wrong or if another blouse is needed, your shopper will run to the appropriate department to fetch the needed item so that you needn't get dressed again. You save time and because you buy much of your wardrobe at once, you have a better chance of it all working well together. Though it seems like an expensive luxury, some women report that they actually save money because they no longer waste time or money on impulse purchases that aren't right.

- Shop by mail. This is especially helpful for items where fit is not important such as scarves and bags.

- Shop alone. While everyone likes support, too many second opinions may encourage you to make purchases you'd never dream of making on your own. It's also a real time-waster when you have your mind set on getting things done.

46

Wardrobe Shopping for Men

Most men would prefer to do anything other than shop for clothing. That's probably why the men's department of most stores is right at street level. Store managers must assume that they're doing well if a man has even stepped in the door, and don't want to push their luck by expecting him to go any further!

While I can't promise that this chapter will make you love shopping, what I can promise is that there is a way to simplify the system and make it as efficient as possible. And remember, the more efficient you are, the less time you'll have to spend at it and the fewer trips you'll have to make!

Planning your wardrobe shopping

- Assess your clothing needs. Most executives find that the following basics meet their needs:
  - three suits – two in plain dark colours, and one in grey or blue in a conservative pattern such as stripes;
  - one navy blue blazer;
  - trousers in grey flannel, khaki and stone (all go with the blue blazer);
  - seven shirts; because the suits and blazer are in basic colours, shop for shirts that co-ordinate with everything. A supply of at least seven shirts allows for one for each day of the business week with a couple left over for travel or for delays at the laundry;
  - an assortment of ties that co-ordinate with the above. (You can vary the look of your outfits by mixing and matching shirts and ties);

- seven pairs of smart socks in grey, black, navy and brown;
- shoes – one black pair, one dark brown.

■ For summer, repeat the basic colours you've chosen for your winter suits, but in lighter fabrics, so that all your shirts and ties will co-ordinate with both your summer and winter wardrobes.

■ As you take stock of your current wardrobe, give away anything that is frayed or beginning to look worn, and discard anything you haven't worn in the last two years.

■ Also note if you are low on underwear or casual clothing, and add those items to your shopping list.

■ Organise your list into categories (casual clothing, work shirts, accessories) to simplify your time in the shop.

■ Set a budget.

Simplifying the shopping trip

■ To avoid confusion about your correct sizes, record your suit size, collar measurement, shoe and hat size, as well as waist and trouser length measurements on an index card to be carried in your wallet. (Give a copy to your mother, wife or girlfriend to guarantee that, from now on, you'll receive presents that fit!)

■ Decide where you would like to shop. Some men prefer to go to one department store and get their shopping done all at one time. Others feel overwhelmed by large stores and prefer to shop at smaller shops.

■ Select shops that fit your image.

■ Shop at a place where the staff are reliable and professional. Try to develop a relationship with a salesperson, as it can save you time and money. That person can call you when a specific raincoat in your size comes in or when the annual sale begins.

■ In order to shop efficiently, it is best to go to the stores at a time when they are least likely to be crowded. The fewer the people, the faster you can be in and out. Listed below, in order of preference, are some possible shopping times:

- a business day right after the store opens;
- just after a store opens on Saturday morning;
- evenings;
- middle of the business day.

What to wear

- Wear clothing appropriate to what you want to buy. If you're buying a blazer, suit or raincoat, be sure to wear a shirt and tie, or a blazer or suit jacket so you can get a feel for how the outfit will look.
- Proper shoes are important for making certain that the trouser length is correct. Proper socks are important if you're buying shoes.
- Go over your list and be sure to take it with you.

What to buy

- Don't buy on impulse. Stick to your list.
- Plan to co-ordinate your entire ensemble on the day you shop for a suit. Buy the tie, the pocket handkerchief, and the shirt that goes with it. It's hard to co-ordinate by trying to remember what you bought, and it's inconvenient to take a suit with you on a future shopping trip.
- Buy classic designs. The clothing lasts, and it won't go out of style as quickly. If you want to look trendy, do it by adding a stylish shirt or tie.
- Don't depend on designer labels. They don't always mean quality.
- Look for quality in make and fabric.
- Try on anything if you're unsure of the fit. It will save you the tedium of having to return it.
- With items such as underwear or sports shirts, buy in bulk if it's a good fit or if the items are on sale.

Wardrobe tips

- If you anticipate having trouble remembering which items can be worn together, set up a coded system showing how your wardrobe can be co-ordinated. Place into groups all garments that go together and assign a letter (A,B,C) to each group. Then mark or sew that letter on the inside label of each garment. (A salesperson might be interested in helping you by listing which items co-ordinate if you buy from him regularly or if you've just bought several co-ordinated purchases.) This system will automatically simplify dressing in the morning.

- Men's wardrobes can benefit by a double row of hanging rods (one high, one lower). One can be for trousers and shirts; the other can hold suits and blazers.

- Use shoe trees to help shoes keep their shape.

- Purchase a tie rack to hang on the back of your wardrobe door. There are many good styles available, so base your decision on what will work well for you. Having your ties conveniently displayed will make neckwear selection easier in the morning.

- Roll underwear, socks and belts for easy storage. (Don't ball socks one inside the other; it stretches out the elastic.)

- A light that goes on as the wardrobe door opens is a handy luxury.

- At the end of the season, check all your clothing for mending or possible discarding. (Old shirts make terrific rags.) Have everything laundered or cleaned before putting it in storage until next season.

Clothing care

- Each night, inspect your suit, shirt and tie for stains, tears, pulls and lost buttons. If repairs are needed, get them done before returning the items to your wardrobe.

- Frequent dry cleaning takes the life out of clothing, so clean only as needed.

- Buy a steamer to take creases and wrinkles out of suits and slacks. It's ideal for home use and perfect for travel.
- Laundries seem to thrive on breaking buttons, so be sure to check your shirt the night before to avoid early-morning panic over a broken button. Keep a supply of extra buttons on hand so that they can be repaired as needed.

PART VII

Children

47

Pregnancy Checklist

The pregnant woman who expects to spend 50 hours a week working, entertaining friends, doing committee work, and still bake home-made bread is making a big mistake. You can do anything, but not everything!

Some women are very fortunate and report having excess energy throughout pregnancy; however, more women find that sometimes they just can't quite keep up with their regular schedule. For some, it comes at the beginning of the pregnancy when morning sickness and an increased need for sleep are common. In my own case (and that of many others), it was the end of pregnancy when I had to slow down. I had made a big effort to get everything done well in advance, and I was so glad I did. Toward the end of my pregnancy, I was confined to bed for a brief period, and I would have been frantic if there had been many things left to take care of. (I will also warn you of what all mothers learn first-hand: with a new baby, it seems you are busy all day, but if you had to describe what occupied all your time, it would either sound silly or it would not sound very time-consuming. But believe me, it is!)

At any rate, you need to start preparing as soon as your pregnancy is confirmed. Your main goal is to be ready when your baby arrives, and that means taking a systematic approach to pregnancy by setting your priorities now – what you want to do; what you need to do.

Here are some ways to handle the many responsibilities ahead.

First trimester

To do

- Make the following decisions about medical care, keeping in mind that each decision will affect the other:

- select the hospital and discuss arrangements with your
  doctor or consultant;
- discuss methods of childbirth with your doctor or
  consultant;
- discuss any testing your doctor recommends.

▪ Start thinking about how to re-arrange your home for the baby.
  Will you need to move or can you manage? Consider your
  options so you'll have time to act before the baby arrives.

▪ Begin a Household Projects page in your Household Notebook
  (see Chapter 23). List anything you want to do to get the house
  in order before the baby is born: re-organise cupboards, clean
  rugs, wax floors, buy washing machine, and so on.

▪ Revise the budget to accommodate the new family member.

▪ Organise family files and records and start a Pregnancy File,
  which includes articles and information on pregnancy, childbirth
  and parenting.

To buy

▪ Select new bras with good support. (You'll want them!)

▪ Buy books on pregnancy, childbirth, breast-feeding and infant
  care.

To call

▪ Call the personnel department of your company and check your
  right to benefits and maternity leave. Some firms require that
  you work until two to four weeks before your due date to qualify
  for benefits.

To enjoy

▪ Take advantage of leisurely weekend mornings and sleep late!

Second trimester

To do

- Many women find this the ideal time to share the good news with family and friends. (Most miscarriages occur in the first trimester, so you're less likely to have problems now.)

- Discuss your preferred maternity leave arrangements with your boss.

- Have amniocentesis, if you plan to do so.

- If you plan to move or remodel, try to complete as much of the project as possible now.

- If you intend to breast-feed, start to prepare your nipples now. Check with your doctor or consult a book on breast-feeding for instructions.

- Most new parents like to have extra assistance when the baby comes. With whom would you feel most comfortable – your mother, sister, a nurse, nanny or mother's help? If you decide on a relative, discuss it now.

- If you plan to employ someone, ask friends for recommendations about individuals or agencies. If you find a real gem, reserve her now. (Most agencies will take bookings on a few days' notice, so you still have plenty of time.)

- If you have other children at home, plan for their care while you'll be in the hospital.

- Borrow any baby clothes you can. Make a list of each item you've borrowed and to whom it belongs. The list will also help you in a few months when you go shopping because you'll know what you don't need to buy. Wash the clothing and put it away.

- Start a presents list, so you can tell people exactly what you want or need when asked.

- Start your list of potential names for the baby.

To buy

- Shop for (or borrow) maternity clothing. Don't forget about a coat or jacket.

To call

- Register for childbirth classes, which will start in your seventh or eighth month.
- Get information on first-aid classes. Knowing emergency procedures is very important in parenting.

To enjoy

- Sneak off for a wonderful holiday with your partner!

Third trimester

To do

- Visit your dentist (don't have any x-rays).
- If you plan to leave work early, make the necessary preparations for a smooth departure.
- Attend childbirth classes with your partner.
- Begin to decorate the baby's room (paint walls, put down carpet, hang curtains, etc.).
- Take a tour of the hospital and maternity ward and learn about the check-in system. (You may also want to ask if you'll be allowed to take photographs in the delivery room.)
- Prepare a list of tasks that will need to be done while you're in the hospital, such as calls to spread the good news and to arrange for deliveries. (Be sure to list all phone numbers!) Also include information your partner may need in order to function at home without you.
- Consider changes to be made in your insurance policies and wills, and choose a guardian for your child. Discuss any changes with your insurance representative and your solicitor, and arrange for them to take effect after the baby's birth.

To buy

- Shop for baby furniture.
- Shop for baby's layette (clothes, cot blankets, accessories).
- Go to the chemist and buy everything the baby may need – a huge stock of nappies, rectal thermometer, baby oil, cotton-wool balls, nappy cream, etc.).
- Buy birth announcement cards, or select some at the printer's and arrange to call the printer when the baby is born. You can get a head start by addressing the envelopes now.

To call

- Check with the hospital about child-care classes and enrol.
- Book a nurse, nanny or mother's help if you haven't already. Give the agency your due date. They'll provide you with someone whether the baby is early or late.
- Call friends for names of potential babysitters.

To enjoy

- Pamper yourself! Get a haircut, enjoy a manicure or facial, or read a good book.

Last month

To do

- Cook ahead and freeze meals for your homecoming.
- Prepare a suitcase for the hospital.
- Prepare a childbirth bag.
- Start interviewing now if you'll need full-time household help when you come home.

To buy

- Buy nursing bras if you plan to breast-feed.

To call
- Confirm child-care arrangements for children at home.

To enjoy
- Celebrate the fact that you are prepared.

At the hospital

To call
- Notify the agency for your nanny or mother's help.
- Give the printer details for the birth announcements, fill in the cards, or phone an announcement in to your chosen newspaper.

48

Post-Pregnancy: Organisation After the Baby is Born

There is no time that is more disorganised or confusing than after coming home with a new baby. There are generally extra people around, no one is following their normal schedule, and everyone is simply basing their actions on what they anticipate the baby's schedule will be – and of course, the little character usually does his or her best to surprise everyone!

Now that I've had twins, I realise how much 'free' time I had when my first-born came along. However, you couldn't have convinced me of that at the time! To cope, I had to develop a way to do all my regular activities, only faster – now I shower more quickly, have a simpler haircut, and do an easier make-up routine. And I had to work out how to do all the child-care chores while still saving time just to be with my baby. It's not easy, but it's possible – eventually.

The art of getting through the early days lies largely in remaining flexible enough to cope with what comes; however, there are some measures you can take to help things along.

If you have not done so already

Ideally, you will have taken care of many of the following points prior to your baby's birth.

- Buy one or two good books on baby care. (Get recommendations from friends.) You won't have time to read many, but they can be reassuring.

- If you're planning to breast-feed, set up a network. Get the number of your local support group and talk to friends who have breast-fed successfully.

- Stock the freezer with breads and pre-cooked dinners for the first days at home.
- Find shops that deliver.
- With your partner's help, prepare a list – complete with phone numbers – of all people who should be called as soon as the baby is born.
- Pre-address announcement envelopes.
- At the office, stay on top of your work, and establish systems so that the staff can run things in your absence.
- Change your will (or have one drawn up) and your insurance policy.

After the birth

- Notify close friends and relatives. To make it simpler, ask some of the first people you call to phone other people with the news.
- Send announcements.

The early days at home

- Don't even attempt to get organised right away. Just do nothing for a while and give yourself time to get back in the swing of things. (Babies don't know about organisation and they really don't care – they just want you to be available when they need you.)
- There's nothing wrong with asking people not to visit immediately. Give yourself time to adjust and rest.
- Accept help from anyone who offers. Don't be afraid to ask for help. This is one time when people are only too glad to lend a hand.
- Relax whenever you can, during the baby's nap or while someone else is with him or her. Only if you are well rested and calm will you be able to enjoy your baby!
- Keep your list of announcements and use it to note down gifts as they arrive. Then tick off each as the thank-you note is sent.

- Write several thank-you notes each day so that doing them doesn't become overwhelming.

- Plan to cook dinners in the morning or arrange for someone else to cook for you.

- Use a shop that delivers, or ask someone to stock up on nappies, formula and food for you.

- Start thinking about what type of household help you might need to employ; evaluate your needs thoroughly before making a decision.

- Arrange with the health visitor for check-ups.

- Arrange an appointment with your own doctor for a check-up (usually at six weeks, but ask your doctor just to be sure).

- Start a photo album and a journal.

- Record your baby's first sounds, including crying, laughing, babbling and cooing.

- Check out support groups for mothers and fathers through your local network and hospitals. Having the opportunity to speak with other parents and share information during this time is very helpful.

- Arrange time for yourself whenever possible. Take the nap time for yourself, and book a temporary babysitter (or call upon a relative or friend) when you need more than an hour or so off.

Starting the day

One of the most common pitfalls new mothers face is finding time to get dressed. I constantly hear, 'And I was still in my nightdress at noon!' Here's what to do.

- If your baby takes an early nap (many go right back to sleep after their first feed), get up and use that time for showering, getting dressed and having breakfast. If you're dressed and feeling somewhat organised, it is easier to face the day. You can use other naps for getting the additional rest you need.

- Not all babies are so co-operative about taking that early nap. Try putting the infant in a baby seat placed on the bathroom floor to watch you shower, dry your hair, and so on. If your baby becomes conditioned to the fact that this is one 10-minute period when you have something else to do, he or she will generally make the most of that time looking around – and plotting how to keep you busy for the rest of the day!

Organising food-related supplies

- If your baby is formula-fed, prepare all the bottles at one time so that you're prepared for the day.
- Always clean the bottles after use so that rotation is easy.
- Store nipples and caps in a closed jar or can so you'll always have pre-sterilised equipment handy. Put used items in another spot (a bowl or another jar) so that you'll know what is ready for sterilising.
- Have one shelf or cupboard for all of the baby's things (bottles, warming dish, spoon, cups).
- In the refrigerator, have one section for baby food so that it's easy to find what's open and available.

Laundry and bath-time tips

- Always keep up with the baby's wash so that you don't run out of babygros, T-shirts, cloths and bibs.
- Have at least three sets of cot sheets: one on the bed, one in the laundry and a fresh one in the drawer.
- Soak clothing immediately after a stain. It's easier to keep it white and fresh that way. (Have a bucket on hand in which to throw soiled items.)
- Select easy-to-wear clothes with poppers in all the important places (for nappy changes and for getting clothes over the baby's head). Once you've tried to dress a screaming baby, you'll be especially glad. Also, always buy big. They grow so quickly!
- Save trips at bath time by using a plastic box with a handle to store baby soap, shampoo, cream, powder and toys.

- Buy canisters meant for storing flour, sugar, and tea to hold baby items (cotton, ribbons, nail scissors, thermometer, etc.).

- For after the bath, put the bottle of baby lotion in hot water. The lotion will be warm when you rub it on the baby's skin.

- Put towels in a tumble dryer for a few minutes just before the bath. It's a wonderful way to get your baby dry!

Getting out of the house

At no time is a parent's organisational skill more sorely tested than when trying to get out of the house with a baby (or a child of any age for that matter!) in tow.

- Always have a pre-packed nappy bag ready to go. Choose one that is soft and featherweight. Velcro fastenings make for easy opening and closing. Outside pockets help you find what you need (baby wipes, tissues, money, or keys) quickly. A vinyl inside makes for easy cleaning. Always re-pack it as soon as you get home. What goes inside? Carry a change of clothing, a blanket, extra formula, a package of nipples and caps, plastic bags with ties for soiled nappies, several sheets of paper towels, wipes and ointment for nappy changes, small bottles of lotion and powder, and at least two extra nappies. Also carry a puppet or some attention-getting toy to get you through a rough time. It sounds like a lot, but it's really not so bad, once you're used to it.

- If you have an appointment, leave an extra 30 minutes for last-minute 'surprises' (and babies will always provide them!), such as an unexpected nappy change or a longer-than-usual feed.

How to get non-baby work done

If you're trying to accomplish something during the early days of motherhood (job search, work-related project, or even finishing thank-you notes), you really can't count on getting much done during the baby's nap. Sleep patterns often change from day to day, and often what you need during that period is a good rest yourself. Here are some suggestions.

- Get back-up help. Consider your needs. Perhaps a babysitter one day a week will be enough, or you may need help three days a week. Establish a set routine with the sitter so that you have one person coming to you regularly. Then the baby will become accustomed to one person, you won't have to re-instruct every time, and you'll know that you will definitely have a specific time to accomplish what needs to be done. Schedule that time, for example:

Monday:	Stay home to work.
Wednesday:	Errands, food shopping, dentist appointment.
Friday:	Stay home to work.

Be consistent or the time will slip away from you.

- Choose an area of the house in which to work where you aren't in sight of the baby, and close the door. Try not to listen. If you've chosen well, your babysitter should be given the authority to handle whatever comes up. If you teach your child that you'll come in at an especially loud wail, he or she will work very hard to produce them.

- Teach your babysitter to schedule and organise. You may need to explain such management techniques as starting the washing machine before going out for a walk with the baby so that the laundry will be finished when she comes back in.

- When you've been out, plan to come home at least 15 minutes before the babysitter has to leave so that you have time to hang up your coat, wash, change clothes and put away your packages; that way, your home won't be in chaos for the rest of the day.

Additional suggestions

- For night feeds, set up a system with your partner so that each of you takes full duty every other night, doing all feeds during that time. That way you each have one full night on, and one full night off for badly needed sleep.

- If you must leave immediately after feeding, get completely ready with make-up, stockings and shoes, but put on a bath robe rather than your clothes. Then you can feed the baby without having to worry about milk getting on the outfit. As soon as you're finished with the feeding, you can slip into your outfit and leave.

■ Consider putting a telephone extension in the baby's room. It can be turned off during naps, and it's certainly handy when the phone rings during a nappy change.

49

Children's Rooms

When it comes to household organisation, one of the most difficult areas to keep well organised is a child's room. Offspring of all ages are experts at creating chaos.

Obviously, picking up after the kids or nagging them is no solution. The first step is to create an environment that is conducive to organisation. This involves letting your children's interests dictate the basic plan for the environment (so that the most interesting items are the most available) and then creating a system that allows your child to help maintain order.

General planning

- The first thing to do is to re-think the use of the child's space and, if necessary, re-arrange it so that his or her interests are taken into consideration. If he loves building bricks but they are difficult to get out and put away, you've automatically created a difficult activity to keep organised. Consider the use of play areas and set up the room accordingly. For your brick builder, create a clear space in a corner of his room and store the bricks near by. If your child is an avid reader, establish a seat near the bookcase and make sure there is good lighting. For a young artist, choose a place where you can put a child's table with art supplies near by. If a three-year-old can take out (and put away) paper and crayons for herself, you've created an effective system.

- I have stressed the importance of colour-coding throughout the book, and nowhere is it more important than in a child's room. There are two practical uses for it:

- in keeping belongings separate. Amanda knows hers are red, so she always knows which toothbrush or towel is hers;

- in putting things away. By using different coloured bins or painting shelves in different colours, you can create a system for your toddler to put toys away. No reading necessary! The dinosaur figures go on the green shelf, the bricks go on the red, and so on.

■ Establish a spot where clutter is allowed on a temporary basis. No child should have to put away everything all the time. If your daughter wants to spread out all the toys from her dolls' house in a pre-established corner of the room, that should be all right for several days. (Set up a system such as Monday and Thursday for cleaning up most projects.) Allow the spot to move occasionally. If the children want to build a card table house in the living room for a night or two and the family won't be inconvenienced, they ought to be able to swap that mess for those in their rooms.

■ For toddlers who mainly play with a variety of big toys, establish baskets or bins in each room in which they can keep a few toys they like to play with. It makes cleaning up in the room much easier, and the bins can be moved easily if you have visitors. In addition, by moving the kitchen bin into the living room occasionally, the children get a whole new perspective on the toys!

■ If your children have their own bedroom as well as playroom, reserve their own rooms for special or new toys. Use the playroom as the main storage area. This simplifies tidying up because everyone knows that all toys go to the playroom.

■ Some families like to establish one room (such as the parents' bedroom) as 'off limits.' While this shouldn't be overdone, it may be workable for some areas. Certainly, most parents should stipulate that because of potential hazards, the bathrooms and areas of the kitchen (such as around the oven) are out of bounds for unsupervised play. Another possibility for preserving a room's tidiness while still allowing your children some freedom might be to stipulate that certain rooms must be used as intended.

Being in the living room is fine if a child wants to sit on the couch with his or her feet on a stool or the floor, but romping and climbing are not allowed.

Storage tips

- Lower hanging poles and hooks in the wardrobe so that your children can reach them. This will make dressing and putting things away much easier.
- Keep toys where they are used. Bath toys should be in a plastic basket in the bathroom; outdoor toys in a shed or by the door.
- Group together similar toys. All puzzles, all games and all stuffed animals should be together.
- Transparent plastic boxes or bins are terrific for storage since the children can see what's in them.
- If you use shelves for storage, make sure they are fastened securely. Bookcases should be anchored as well. Active toddlers are prone to scaling any type of shelving.
- Mesh laundry bags make terrific toy sacks for large, awkward items. They're see-through so there is no problem with identification, and it's a good way to keep all parts of a toy together.
- Use sketches or a catalogue photograph taped to a box to identify certain items. Children too young to read can easily identify the 'beads' box if it has a picture of beads on the outside.
- Are jigsaw puzzle pieces constantly getting mixed up? When they get a new puzzle, assign it a number and write that number on the back of each piece and on the box. When a piece is found, you'll know exactly in which box it goes.
- For an infant's toys or for a toy that has a lot of pieces, collect the toys (or pieces) on a sheet on which the child can play. When the child is done, simply fold up the sheet – toys and all – and put it away for the next time.

■ Encourage children to get out only a few toys at a time. If they want to do puzzles, encourage them to put away the game first.

Weeding out

■ Automatically throw away any toy that becomes dangerous. If a part snaps off and there's a sharp edge, or if eyes on a stuffed animal cannot be secured and might come off and cause a child to choke, throw it away.

■ Until your child is old enough to take care of his or her own room and keep it tidy, you have the right to weed things out periodically. After all, the clay sculpture her best friend gave her six months ago and the Barbie shoe whose pair is missing really can't be saved for ever.

■ Give your child the chance to make the decision to part with a toy. If you've noticed one that hasn't been used in awhile, you might ask if it's all right to give it away to a hospital or charity shop). Sometimes a child will surprise you with a 'yes'. If your child is a hoarder and is going to make it impossible for you ever to give or throw anything away, wait a few months or a year before asking permission again. For the time being, you'd better make the decisions yourself.

■ If a part is lost (and it's not such a favourite toy that you are met with a flood of tears until you promise to replace the part), use that as a reason to throw a toy out.

■ Favourite toys can often be fixed. Some cities have doll 'hospitals'. For other types of toy, contact your local toy shop or the manufacturer.

■ Suggest that your child should give away one toy when he or she receives a new one.

■ Let your child help pack toys in a box for charity; talk about how happy another child will be to receive them.

■ Rotate toys. If your child just can't part with some toys but you need to clear space, establish a 'surprise' bin and cycle some of the toys out for a while. Then, if your child is ill at home or you feel trapped inside on a rainy day, you can pull out the bin. You'll probably both be in for a surprise at how much fun your child will have playing with the old toys. (If any toy doesn't catch the child's interest after being taken out of circulation for awhile, throw it out.)

■ Exchange toys. Perhaps your child and his friend would like to swap games, puzzles or books for a time. Specify a date when the toys should be returned; trading for 'keeps' is hard at almost any age.

50

Teaching Children About Organisation

Parents who teach their children an organisational system and the value of it will have given them a head start in life. The toddler will begin to learn responsibility and be better prepared to cope with the 'putting away' rules of nursery school. And as the child matures, he or she will be learning some basic organisational skills that will help build life-long work habits.

As a youngster, it never dawned on me that people could be dis-organised. I thought everyone knew where their shoes, socks, toys and books were; what time school began; when their homework was due; and so on. By the time I was ten I had determined that to save time in the morning, I could put my packed satchel by the front door the night before so that when it was time to leave in the morning, all I had to do was grab it and run. I suppose I was just better organised than anyone else, and it has helped me throughout my life.

Organisation is a skill that can be learned. The earlier you start instilling in your children these habits and the benefits, the easier it will be for them.

With toddlers, the place to start is by having them help with the day-to-day tidying up of toys. As they grow older, you'll want to teach them how to be responsible for their own room and ask them to help with specific tasks around the house. This will help promote a feeling of self-reliance and give them more control over their lives. Another important benefit of good organisational habits is when it comes to schoolwork.

Cleaning up, toddler-style

Toddlers should learn that what comes out must go back. There are fun ways to encourage your child to help and still allow you to get the job done efficiently.

- Encourage your child to help with tidying up, but don't overwhelm him or her. Request help with just one thing at a time. 'You pick up the doll's clothes; I'll do the books.'

- Sing while you work together.

- Ask, 'How quickly do you think we can we get this done?' Set the kitchen timer for five or ten minutes and see if you can get everything done before the bell rings.

- Make a game of it. Ask, 'Can you pick up all the stuffed animals and put them back before I finish with the bricks?'

As they grow – taking responsibility for their own rooms

- Simplify a task according to age level. Teach a toddler how to make a bed by standing at the head of the bed and pulling up the covers.

- Establish a standard so that your child knows what is expected. For example, you may care only that your eight-year-old pulls the duvet over the bed, not that the sheets underneath are wrinkle-free. Tell your child exactly what is expected.

- Involve your children in your efforts by taking them shopping with you for boxes and bins for storage. Let them help choose the colours and styles.

- Label where everything goes (via colour-coded or written labels) so that your child knows what goes where.

- Assign a special drawer or shelf in the bathroom for their belongings.

- Suggest ways to get the job done pleasantly by putting on a favourite CD, telling yourself a story, pretending to be Cinderella, and so on.

- Have a laundry basket in the child's room, and make him or her responsible for putting dirty clothes there. At a later date, you can teach children to be responsible for putting away as well. Show them how you want the clothes placed and in what drawers, but don't expect perfection!

- Help children build personal pride in their room. Let them have a hand in decorating it and praise them for the times when they are showing an interest in beautifying it (despite the fact that the two of you may have a different definition of 'beauty!').

- Children usually get attention for not cleaning their room. Be sure to pay attention when they do.

Taking on other responsibilities

- Set an example of planning and priorities by talking in those terms about everyday household events. For example, a child who can read can help plan a trip to the grocery store by looking through a recipe and listing those ingredients that must be purchased.

- Getting an older child to do household chores usually involves constant reminding. You can establish a chart to help your child determine what he or she is supposed to do on a given day. A chart should list each family member's name, followed by the tasks for which he or she is currently responsible, and the day on which each is to be done. (Note that each person gets a free day occasionally.)

	Mon.	Tues.	Wed.	Thurs.	Fri.	Sat.	Sun.
Mum	dishes	FREE	rubbish	dusting	set table	dishes	FREE
Dad	dusting	dishes	FREE	rubbish	FREE	set table	dishes
Amanda	FREE	set table	dishes	pick up main rooms	rubbish	FREE	set table
Elizabeth	rubbish	FREE	set table	dishes	wipe counters	rubbish	FREE
Julia	rubbish	FREE	dishes	set table	dishes	dusting	FREE

■ Alternatively, a job dial can be made by cutting out two cardboard circles, one larger than the other. The large circle records the tasks to be done (take responsibility for the dishes, set the table, take out the rubbish); the smaller circle notes each family member's name.

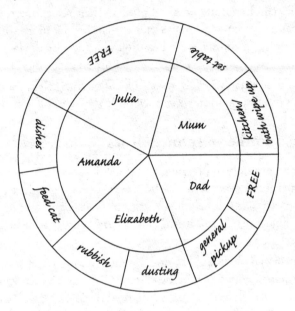

Using a paper fastener, the two are put together, circle upon circle. (The larger circle is stationary, the smaller one turns.) Every day the smaller dial is moved one position to the right. Then each family member is responsible for the task that appears adjacent to his or her name.

■ As your children mature, let them take charge of marking their own dates on the family calendar. You're the best judge of when each is ready for that responsibility.

■ Check with your child about upcoming events at school so that no one misses a date because a note was lost. (The child is responsible, but you offer a system of cross-checking.)

Teaching self-reliance

I once met a friend's daughter who was very self-sufficient, even aged six. I visited her family one day when my daughter was five months old, and she was always one step ahead of me – getting out a fresh nappy, feeding the baby her cereal, and pushing the pushchair. Young children can do a lot!

- Both mother and father should play active roles in the tidying up and organisational work of the home. The best way to teach is by example.

- Help children become more independent by teaching them how to tie their shoes, button their coat, get their own snack, or operate the video player. The more they can do, the better they'll feel about themselves, and the more organised you can be.

Schoolwork and organisation

As a child begins to assume responsibility for schoolwork, organisation becomes more important than ever. The children who learn how to arrange their books, desks, satchels and exercise books are more likely to become organised adults.

- For schoolwork, provide your child with a well-lit, comfortable work area.

- Suggest that your child should establish a colour-coding system for homework folders by subject. Most children enjoy a trip to the stationery store to buy the necessary supplies, and the system will help them throughout the year.

- Teach your child how to label notebooks and arrange desk supplies.

- When you first see your child after school, ask about homework and discuss what they have to do and how long it should take. You can help them set up a time management system. If necessary, you can establish a reward such as 'After you finish you can watch half an hour of television.'

- If your child seems stuck, stop and help him or her plan steps to complete something (break a large task down into parts, etc.).
- Praise your child for work well done. Talk about what great progress he or she is making in developing positive work habits for later in life.

51

Travelling with Children

While the hours you spend on a plane or in a car with your child may not be the highlight of your life, remember what someone once said: All places should be seen through a child's eyes. After all, it is the children who stop to notice the small details, and it is they who take the time to sit by a fountain rather than rushing from one museum to another.

If you're brave enough to pack your youngsters and go, chances are you'll have a wonderful time.

General planning

- If possible, plan to travel during the child's nap time.
- Think through your child's day and make a checklist so you won't forget certain 'must have's' (blanket, wipes, etc.). One woman I know had made a great list of clothing and bedding needs but had neglected to include the everyday items such as nappies, dummies, and bottles. Sure enough, she forgot the bottles – they were in the steriliser!
- Let one person do the packing. One mother assumed her husband had packed the baby food and the bottles, and they were both distressed to discover that he hadn't.
- Take at least one full change of clothes in case of spills or travel sickness. (The younger the child, the more clothes you are likely to need. For an infant, take along two or three changes – the second set of backup clothes can be lightweight so they are easy to pack, and you can add a jumper if it's chilly.) Pack separates when possible. That way if the shirt gets juice all over it, at least you don't have to change the trousers.

- Expect the unexpected. If you'll be in the car or on the plane for five hours, take enough nappies for ten to fifteen hours. (In your suitcase, be sure to pack nappies for your arrival so you don't immediately have to head for the shops.)

- Take an adequate supply of plastic bags for nappies and rubbish. A nervous child can develop diarrhoea, and you don't want to be caught short without a way to dispose of the nappies!

- Take any and all medications your child might need. Colds are a particular worry when travelling, so take along the remedies your doctor recommends. And if your child has a tendency to any illness, such as ear infections, also take any medication the doctor may have prescribed. There's nothing worse than being in a strange city and not having the necessary medicine in the middle of the night. Remember, anticipate the unexpected.

- For very young children, pack familiar toys and books so there will be something to give them the feeling of home. Ideally, pack these toys (all but the true favorites) about a week in advance so that they seem new but familiar at the same time. A few new toys are nice, but there's no need to over do it. For entertainment at your destination, blow-up toys are wonderful because they pack so easily.

- If you're comfortable with your baby in a frontpack (or backpack) baby carrier or a sling, be sure to plan on travelling with it. It makes you far more mobile than having to totally rely on using a pushchair.

- If your child is under three, invest in a toddler seat that attaches to the table (collapsible models are now available). Not all restaurants have highchairs, so having one along will make meals much more manageable. If you're travelling by plane, pack the seat in the bottom of your suitcase; if travelling by car, put it in an accessible spot in the boot in case you need it en route.

- Buy a travel clothesline or clothes horse so that you can wash light clothing by hand and hang to dry.

- If you are going away on business, bring a relative or babysitter to help out or arrange for one at your destination.

- Select a family-oriented hotel. If you're travelling to a foreign country, make certain that you'll have your own bath, and try to clarify what they mean by certain words such as 'suite'. One family expected a separate bedroom for the children and discovered that the bedroom was an alcove that couldn't be darkened unless everyone in the family went to bed at the same time.

- When you reserve your room, ask for a cot, if needed, and inquire about a babysitting service. If a hotel regularly serves families, you can have some degree of confidence in the service, as the hotel wouldn't recommend it if they received complaints. If you have any concerns, ask for and check references.

- If you're travelling to a foreign country, tell your doctor where you're going. His or her advice will make your trip a smoother one. Also check regarding immunisations.

Planning for a plane trip

- When possible, book seats in advance so that all family members will be together. Tell them if a non-paying infant will be sharing one of the seats. They will generally try to save a seat next to you unless the plane is 100 per cent full. When you get to the airport, remind the ticket agent that you are travelling with an infant and would like a seat held if possible.

- If your child will need any medication during the trip or straight after, be sure to carry it on board with you in case your bags are lost.

- Select a carry-on bag made of lightweight material, and choose one with lots of outside pockets for greater accessibility. You will want to pack as much as you need without overdoing it. Heavy carry-on luggage is a real nuisance. Keep in mind that you may be carrying:
  - Nappies, plastic bags, wipes, nappy rash cream
  - Food
  - Medicine

- Extra clothes, blankets, jumpers
- Toys, games, books

- Expect that there may be variations in cabin temperature so all family members should dress in layers they can add and take off as needed.
- If friends or relatives will be waiting at your destination, you may want to pack one special outfit in your hand luggage so that you can change the child just before arrival.

Travel and food

- With plane travel, phone ahead to find out what the special child's meal is, and if it's something he or she likes, reserve it for your youngster.
- Be overprepared when it comes to food. One mother spent an additional five hours on a plane with her infant, but fortunately she was carrying enough formula to get through.
- Don't expect that the aeroplane meal will really be your child's regular meal. If the plane is delayed, 'lunch' may be served at 4 p.m., so pack enough substantial food that your child can use the plane meal as entertainment, not nourishment.
- If your child is particular, take along lots of whatever you think might not be available where you are going (e.g., juices in America are different, so you may want to take your own).
- For any type of travel, food is a real help. Raisins and crisps are easy and fun. Pack in plastic food-storage bags so you can throw them away when you've finished.

On board

- Try to avoid checking in your collapsible stroller. Carrying an infant or child in addition to your hand luggage is just too much – especially if there are delays and you are stranded at an airport for several hours.

- Having something to suck on during take-off and landing will help your child's ears adjust to the changes in air pressure. Breastfeeding or a bottle (or lollipops for an older child) can help get them through this time.
- Some families like the bulkhead seats because those rows offer more leg room; however, there are disadvantages. You often have to give up your hand luggage during take-off and landing since there is no nearby storage available for it. In addition, you sometimes must rely on the flight attendant to set up tray tables. Thus, many families prefer to be part of a normal row where the children can control their own tray table to eat or play games when they like.
- If travelling alone with a baby, avoid getting a centre seat. If you are booked for one on a full flight, a flight attendant can generally work out a swap for you. People do have sympathy!
- Ask the flight attendant for any items the children might enjoy, perhaps a deck of cards or model of the aeroplane.

At the hotel

- If you are in a foreign country, have bottled water sent to your room.
- Check the hotel cot for sturdiness. Be certain that the sides lock firmly into a raised position.
- Ask for four to six large towels to roll up and use as cot bumpers.
- Babyproof the hotel room. Go over it on your hands and knees to evaluate what your child might get into. Travel with plug guards (in foreign countries you may need to use tape) and bring tape for sharp corners and edges. Ask that any glass tables be removed.

Travelling with older children

- Older children love the new and unexpected. Visit a toy shop and pick up activity books, games, and crossword puzzles for the trip.

- If you travel frequently, make a travel art-and-activity bag. Keep it permanently packed with paper, crayons, scissors, stickers, stars, an activity book, and mazes. It's easier than packing a new one every time, and it gives a child something specific to look forward to.

- Make tapes of CDs (or record your own stories). If travelling by car, you can play them in the tape deck. If traveling by plane, bring a tape player with ear phones.

- Let your child pack his or her own small bag of special belongings, perhaps in an easy-to-carry backpack. A child as young as three will enjoy the importance of being able to pack for him- or herself. Check it once it's packed; your child may have created a bag that weighs a ton, and you'll want to help him or her be a bit more realistic about what should go with you. However, remember that you can't rely on those items to keep your youngster busy for the trip. You'll need to pack special items for entertainment.

- When you get to the place you're visiting, try to contact other families. Many children are rejuvenated by seeing other youngsters.

- Ask about local playgrounds. An hour at one can often wear off enough of a child's excess energy that the family can devote the rest of the day to sightseeing.

When I look back on my childhood, the warmest memories I have are the family holidays we had. Even ten-hour car journeys (and I got carsick!) were happy times for me. I loved travelling with my parents and enjoyed those special times of being with them. So while you pack an unending supply of nappies and toys and games, just remember that it will almost certainly pay off for your family in the long run!

52

When Travel Means Leaving the Children Behind

When one or both parents must go away, it's difficult for the entire family. Parents are under stress to make all the family arrangements, and children are concerned about missing their parents for a time. Even if only one parent is away, family dynamics change, and children keenly feel a parent's absence.

I learned first hand the importance of preparing the family for our absence. A year ago my husband and I were just returning home from our first trip in 10 years without the children, and as we pulled into the drive at 10 p.m., we were alarmed to see our neighbour standing in the doorway. One of our three-year-old twins, who had just started sleeping in a big bed, had fallen out of the bed and had got a deep cut above his eye. Following my written 'in case of emergency' instructions, the child-minder had called the neighbour to come and look after the other children while she took our son to casualty. My neighbour said to me, 'I couldn't believe it. Your child-minder was so prepared. She had your list and emergency envelope in her hand when I arrived, and she knew just what to do.'

While you will rarely return to find that the family has encountered a true emergency, there are many measures to take that will lessen your worries and keep the house running smoothly while you're away.

Making special preparations

- Children should be told ahead of time. For a business trip, little ones need just a few days' notice; children seven and older can be told a week or two in advance. Tell them where you're going, why, and when you'll be back. Even a toddler should get a clear explanation.

- You can share your trip with your children by pointing out on a map where you're going and talking a bit about what you expect (or know) it will be like: 'New York is huge city. If I look out the window during my meeting, I'll see some of the tallest buildings you can imagine. Maybe one day we'll go there on holiday together.'

- With small children, create a visual way of explaining how long you'll be gone. Using an ordinary notebook, make your own page-a-day diary that the child-minder or your partner can review with them each morning. For each day that you'll be gone, write or sketch what they'll be doing on the bottom of the page, and what you'll be doing at the top. Continue this on each page representing a day you'll be gone. Perhaps the page for the day after you return could show all of you doing something special together.

- Leave a special sticker or a small piece of candy for each day you're away. By seeing how many treats they have left until you return, they'll have a method for measuring time. You can combine this with your page-a-day trip diary by attaching the special treat to each page.

- For children seven and older, mark the family wall calendar with the days of your absence. In addition, you can create a child-orientated itinerary for older children to read. We put a 'happy face' on our wall calendar to mark the day of our return, and the twins take turns putting a big red 'X' on each day as it passes.

- Plan special activities for the children while you're away. Arrange for them to visit friends, or ask Grandma to take them out to the cinema.

- Record stories, messages or songs for your children to listen to each night while you're gone. (Stories or songs recorded on tape can be put away for use during the next trip.)

- If the stay is indefinite (helping a family member through an illness, for example), over-estimate the time you'll be gone.

- Explain to the children relevant instructions that you've left with the child-minder: 'I've told Aunt Mary you can watch an extra half an hour of television on Friday night, but otherwise I expect you to follow the usual rules.'

- If lifts to school will change because of your absence, tell the children what to expect.

- Will you miss a significant event such as a play or a concert? Ask the teacher if you may come to a dress rehearsal instead.

- If you travel regularly, establish a going-away ritual. With a toddler it might be going out for ice cream the night before you leave; older children might prefer playing a game. Even teenagers look forward to something special like a dinner out.

- If your child is going through a difficult time, you might try to postpone the trip, shorten it by a day or two, or even bring the child with you. If none of these solutions is workable, tell your child that you really must go, and then promise a special treat for the two of you when you return.

Household organisation

Assembling important information

- The person in charge of your children while you are away should have:

  - complete medical information on each child: for example history of ear infections, allergies, special diet, any medication;

  - list of important telephone numbers such as the doctor, the chemist, the vet, a relative, the school, etc.;

  - a detailed day-to-day schedule (see below) of where you'll be, complete with phone numbers of hotels and offices, and dates and times; flight information, with phone numbers of airlines. If the weather is bad or there is a reason for a delay, those left at home can check your flight progress throughout the day.

ITINERARY	
Monday, 28 September	
7.00 pm:	BA123 London Heathrow to New York (BA information: 01234 987 654)
7.30 pm (local time):	Arrive New York. Going straight to hotel: Intercontinental Hotel (001 212 555-1234).
Tuesday, 29 September	
12 noon:	Lunch at Smith & Stone Advertising (001 212 555-4321). In emergency, leave message with Sarah Jones.
2.30 pm:	To conference. Paging number: 001 212 555-6543.
5.00–7.30 pm:	At hotel.
7.30 pm:	Conference dinner in Intercontinental ball-room.

Houshold organisation – assembling detailed lists

- Your child-minder or babysitter should be left with a complete list of what is to be done each day. If it's a regular person who knows the general routine, write the extra activities or chores on Post-it notes that can be attached to the calendar on the appropriate day. As the task gets done, the note gets thrown away.

- If the person doesn't know the household well, you'll need two lists. One will be the basics of household management and should be general enough to last for a year or two of absences. The other list provides your children's schedules, including specific information about meals, homework and arrangements such as visits to friends.

- To create these lists, take a day or two to observe exactly how the day flows.

- Always review these lists with the person involved to make sure there are no questions.

HOUSEHOLD MANAGEMENT LIST

Monday

7 am: Feed dog 3 biscuits.

Tidy kitchen after breakfast.

Sweep floor.

Change beds.

Check grocery list; pick up any necessary items.

5 pm: Feed dog one bowl dry food, 2 biscuits.

Prepare school lunches after dinner.

Run dishwasher.

Empty dishwasher; lay out breakfast dishes.

Tuesday

7 am: Feed dog 3 biscuits.

Tidy kitchen after breakfast.

Start laundry; fold and put away.

5 pm: Feed dog one bowl of dry food, 2 biscuits.

Prepare school lunches after dinner.

Run dishwasher.

Empty dishwasher; lay out breakfast dishes.

CHILDREN'S SCHEDULE	

Monday, 28 September

6.45 am	Wake Heather (dresses herself).
7.10	Wake Charlie – help him get dressed.
7.30	Breakfast (Heather: orange juice, cereal, and toast; Charlie: milk, muffin, and apple slices).
8.05	Bus comes for Heather. (She should have her backpack and lunch; sweater if it's chilly.)
8.45	Drive Charlie to nursery school.
12.00 pm	Nursery school pick-up. Jamie coming to play. Mother: Susan Miller, 833 221. She'll pick up Jamie about 2.30.
3.40	Meet Heather's bus.
4.15–4.30	Heather should start homework. May need you to sit with her. Generally spends about 30 minutes on it.
5.30	Bath time. Make sure Heather washes her hair and dries it well.
6.00	Dinner. Lasagne in the refrigerator.
8.00	Charlie goes to bed. (Brush teeth.) He gets two stories and must have his stuffed monkey. If you can't find it, check the kitchen cupboard where I keep pots—he often hides it there.
8.15	Heather gets in bed. We read for 15 minutes, then lights out.

- If you were leaving a baby, you would note all feedings and the amounts given. A complete schedule for the morning might look like this.

BABY'S MORNING SCHEDULE	
7.00 am	Baby wakes; change nappy.
7.30	Breakfast
	3 teaspoons mashed bananas
	3 teaspoons rice cereal
	7 oz. formula
8.00	One dropper baby vitamins; clean up and put into clothes.
9.00	Morning walk (don't forget sunblock and hat)
10.00–11.30	Nap
12.00 pm	Lunch
	Strained vegetables (peas or sweet potatoes)
	Apple
	7 oz. formula

Household organisation – helpful tips

- The more routine the children's lives are while you're gone, the better. Try not to change babysitters just before a trip, and while it's nice to let the sitter offer a few special privileges, the children are better off sticking with the rules and knowing what the limits are.
- If the person with whom you are leaving the children is an unpaid relative, or a babysitter covering for more than a week, set up a support system to help them. Consider budgeting for a teenager to help out a couple of afternoons while you're away. Also ask the children to pitch in: help with their lunches and meals, do dishes, feed pets, etc.

- Ask a neighbour or a relative to drop in both announced and unannounced. The feedback you receive should give you peace of mind.

If your child stays elsewhere while you are away

Perhaps Grandma has offered to help with the kids, but they'll be at her house for the first time, not yours. Here are some ideas.

- Talk with your children about other 'firsts' at which they have succeeded.
- Visit Grandma's house first and talk about some of the things that will happen when the children stay there.
- If a visit isn't possible, arrange for photographs to be taken to show (or remind) children of what it's like.
- Leave your relative with emergency information, the page-a-day diary you created, and a copy of your children's schedule, including exactly when you'll pick them up. While you certainly don't want to dictate their day, Grandma should know meal-times, as well as nap and bedtimes so that the basic daily routine can remain the same. You should also give them a list of telephone numbers of friends, as well as details of any arrangements for lifts to school.
- Talk of the experience as a double adventure: your business trip and their stay at Grandma's, for example.

While you are away

- In advance, agree a time when you'll phone each day. If possible, call at the same time so that a new ritual comes into play.
- Phone at the appointed hours. Don't be alarmed if your child cries while on the phone (or refuses to speak to you). It's his or her chance to unbottle some feelings, and as long as the minder reports that things are going well, you needn't be over-concerned.

- If you do speak with your children, don't get involved in any heated discussions. Expressing anger or disappointment about something that happened when you're not there leaves a child with a difficult set of emotions to handle on his or her own.
- Don't let the conversation be one-sided. Let them know how you're doing and what's going on.

Preparing for your return

- If your trip was for business, try to get related memos, letters, follow-up and thank-you notes written before you return. Do it at night in the hotel room or on the plane coming home.
- Should you bring a gift? Of course. It needn't be expensive. It's another ritual for the children to anticipate, and it eases the pain of separation.
- Don't come home feeling compelled to 'set everything right'. Ask family members to pitch in with any family task that must be attended to, and otherwise, catch up with home chores gradually so that you can spend the time with the children.
- If you feel you must go right back to the office the first morning home, try to come home from work an hour earlier that day.
- On your return, do something special as a family. The first weekend you're home, set aside some time for family as well as for catching up on work and/or home chores.

An occasional alternative: taking the kids along

- If you or your partner travel frequently, consider taking your children along sometimes and leaving them with a hotel babysitter while you're busy during the day. One lawyer takes just one of his children with him when schedules permit, providing a special time for both child and parent.
- Make yourself available periodically during the day, even if it's meeting for half an hour at lunch-time before you return to your meeting. If you're going to be in back-to-back meetings or under extreme pressure, take your child another time.

- Call the hotel to see what family services are offered. Some hotels have playgrounds, pools and babysitting services.
- If you're renting a car, request a car seat, if needed.
- Book a room with a refrigerator. It's much easier (and less expensive) to feed children if you can keep milk and cheese and other favourites in the room with you.
- Maintain your child's normal sleeping and eating patterns as much as possible while you're away.
- Sightseeing can make your trip one that both of you will remember for a long time to come. Those special business trips will make up for all the ones where you have to leave the children behind!

ABOUT THE AUTHORS

Ronni Eisenberg is a time management and organisational expert in the USA. She has run organising workshops and has lectured on time management for major corporations and national business associations. In addition, she frequently does one-on-one consulting regarding organisation in the workplace.

Ronni Eisenberg has also served as spokesperson for several major consumer product campaigns and created her own line of organising products.

Kate Kelly, a professional writer, is the author of *The Complete Idiot's Guide to Parenting a Teenager* and *Election Day: An American Holiday, An American History*. She has also co-authored a book on home re-modelling, *Renovating with a Contractor*, and has ghostwritten several other titles.

In addition to *Organise Yourself!*, Ronni Eisenberg and Kate Kelly together have written four other books: *The Overwhelmed Person's Guide to Time Management, Organise Your Office!, Organise Your Home!*, and *Organise Your Family!*

If you would like to write to comment on the book or send in your organising suggestions, please write to Ronni Eisenberg & Associates, P.O. Box 3272, Westport, CT 06880, USA.

STORAGE

~~Spare Room~~ - Dressing Up Box.

(in same bag!) { Blow-Up Bed
{ Hammock

Wooden Chest - Small wicker basket